Slovenia

Front cover: Ribčev Laz village, Lake Bohinj

Right: Ljubljana's Dragon Bridge has a dragon on each corner

TOP 10 ATTRACTIONS

Lake Bled • A magical, glacial lake in the northwest surrounded by rugged, snowcapped mountains and forested slopes *(page 38)*

Lipica Stud Farm • The home of the famous Lipizzaner horses *(page 55)*

Koper old town • The medieval quarter of Slovenia's main port has many beautiful buildings *(page 58)*

Piran • Inspired by Venice, it is the loveliest town on the coast *(page 60)*

ča Valley • Its rocky
rges are the place to go
r outdoor sports *(page 46)*

Ljubljana • The friendly, easy-going capital makes a good starting point for any tour *(page 27)*

stojna and Škocjan Caves • Take trips to the underground
arvels of the Karst region *(pages 53 and 55)*

Wine roads • Cellar visits and tastings are on offer in the northeast *(page 73)*

ke Bohinj • Surrounded by the wild Triglav National Park,
is is a great area for walking and adventure sports *(page 42)*

Rogaška Slatina • The country's oldest and most-visited spa town *(page 67)*

A PERFECT DAY

9.00am Breakfast

Start the day with breakfast at your hotel, then head for Prešerenov trg. If you would prefer breakfast in a café, a few yards east of the square along Petkovskovo nabrezje, is Café Promenada where the outside tables have great views over the river.

10.00am The market and the cathedral

Cross Triple Bridge (Tromostovje) and turn left along the river. Visit the cathedral, Plečnik's Central Market (go downstairs for the fish market) and Dragon Bridge. Then take a stroll through the main market square.

11.00am Castle climb

From Krekov trg on the far side of the market, take the funicular railway up to the Castle. Climb up the Observation Tower for great views across the city.

1.00pm A spot of lunch

For something up-market, the Castle restaurant serves high-class Slovenian cuisine. For a popular local snack, try *burek* (Bosnian-style pastry filled with cheese or meat) from a stall on the market (head for the southeast corner), and there are plenty of cafés in Old Ljubljana.

2.00pm See the sights

Follow Ciril-Metodov trg past the Cathedral and into medieval Old Ljubljana. Wander along as far as Gornji trg, window-shopping as you go. Cross Shoemaker's Bridge and find your way to the charming Trg francoske revolucia. Look into Plečnik's Summer Theatre, then stroll up Vegova ulica, passing Baroque buildings and the National Library to Kongresni trg.

IN LJUBLJANA

6.00pm An evening stroll

In summer, take the underpass under the busy road and stroll through Tivoli Park. Or at any time of year return to the Ljubljanica and find a café for an early evening drink. In December, there is a Christmas market on the east side of the river, south of the Triple Bridge.

10.30pm On the town

For an after-dinner drink, head for bars on the east bank of the Ljubljanica, between Triple Bridge and Shoemakers' Bridge, Maček is the oldest and most famous. For atmospheric alternative nightlife, head for Metelkova, a complex of clubs, bars and galleries in a disused army barracks *(see page 95)*.

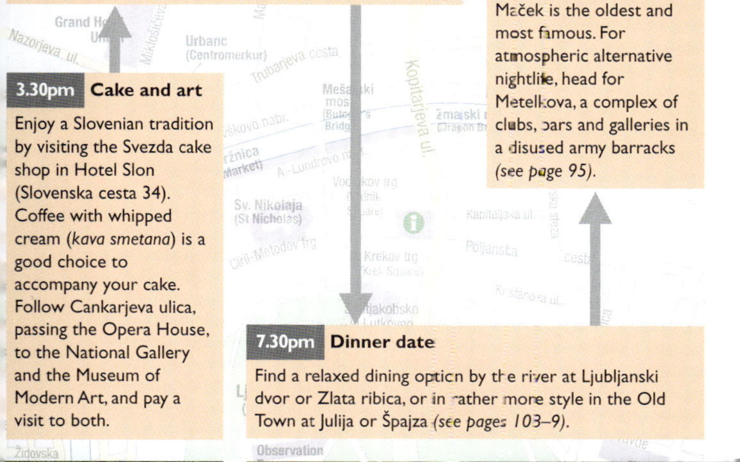

3.30pm Cake and art

Enjoy a Slovenian tradition by visiting the Svezda cake shop in Hotel Slon (Slovenska cesta 34). Coffee with whipped cream (*kava smetana*) is a good choice to accompany your cake. Follow Cankarjeva ulica, passing the Opera House, to the National Gallery and the Museum of Modern Art, and pay a visit to both.

7.30pm Dinner date

Find a relaxed dining option by the river at Ljubljanski dvor or Zlata ribica, or in rather more style in the Old Town at Julija or Špajza *(see pages 103–9)*.

35

32

87

CONTENTS

Features

92

8

83

INTRODUCTION

Tiny Slovenia, no bigger than Wales, is a Central European country lying between Italy to the west, Austria to the north, Hungary to the east and Croatia to the southeast. With a 47km (29-mile) coastal strip lapped by a turquoise sea, snow-capped Alpine mountains rising more than 2,500m (8,200ft), tree-clad hills and fertile plains, it is gifted with astounding regional variation. It is also culturally rich, sitting on a corner of the Adriatic Sea at the edge of both Western Europe and the Balkan Peninsula. But the country's greatest attractions are undoubtedly its dramatic landscapes and unspoilt natural features, which make a splendid playground for those who enjoy the outdoor life and adventure sports.

'See you soon'

Natural Playground

Slovenia knows how to capitalise on these assets, and visitors will find excellent leisure and sports facilities wherever they go. Almost half the country is covered with forest, while much of the remainder is given over to pastures, arable land, orchards and vineyards. The Alpine northwest is dominated by the tall, jagged mountains and peaceful green valleys of Triglav National Park in the Julian Alps, which is criss-crossed by a network of clearly signed hiking trails. Traditional, low-impact farming methods have meant that the remote mountains remain havens for wild animals such as brown bears, wolves, boar, deer, chamois and lynx.

Winter snowfall in the mountains is substantial, and locals head for the well-equipped ski resorts with hire facilities and ski schools. In summer, the picturesque lakes of Bled and Bohinj offer the chance to swim in pristine water or rent a rowing boat. Close by, the River Soča is the place for watersports such as rafting, kayaking, canoeing and hydrospeed, as well as canyoning and trout fishing. There are also a number of well-maintained golf courses. For those with transport, the Tourist Board has devised several wine roads, leading through rural landscapes to vineyards and cellars that offer wine tasting and the chance to buy direct from producers.

Škocjan Caves, a huge hollow in the Karst mountains

Although Slovenia possesses only a small stretch of seaboard, the coast has been carefully developed, with three modern yachting marinas and several pleasant beaches, as well as high-class hotels and an abundance of seafood restaurants. Inland, the Karst region is known for its dramatic limestone caves clustered with stalagmites and stalactites, two of which are artificially lit and open to the public for guided tours.

In eastern Slovenia, which is flatter and more fertile,

spas cater to both the infirm and the indulgent fit. The classic 19th-century Austro-Hungarian spa towns must now compete with 21st-century minimalist resorts that have recreational water parks and wellness centres for pampering breaks. For closer contact with the country, visitors should consider the agrotourism centres scattered throughout Slovenia. These offer the chance to eat and sleep in a working farm environment.

Lepena Valley – almost half the country is covered with forest

Climate

The clearly defined geographic regions are matched by climatic differences. The mountains in the northwest have an alpine climate with warm summers and cold winters when snowfall is heavy; the coast to the southwest has a Mediterranean climate with hot, sunny summers and pleasant, mild winters; and the inland region to the east has a Continental climate with hot, dry summers and cold winters. In summer, it is not unusual for temperatures to rise above 30°C (86°F). In winter, the coast seldom sees temperatures fall below freezing, but in the mountains they can drop to –20°C (–4°F).

Consequently, Slovenia has two main tourist seasons: summer, from late May to early October, when it is warm enough to swim, and winter, from mid-December to late March, when it is possible to ski and snowboard. Spring or autumn, when it is neither too hot nor too cold, are the best times for hiking, cycling and other outdoor sports.

The Cooperative Bank in Ljubljana, in Viennese Secessionist style

Population

The largest city is the capital, Ljubljana, which has a population of 330,000. There are no other large cities, but many towns have well-preserved historic centres, decent hotels and a friendly, relaxed atmosphere where life is lived outdoors in cafés and in authentic restaurants. Architecturally, the most interesting old towns are Ljubljana, Maribor and Ptuj, where the Baroque style predominates, and the coastal settlements of Koper and Piran, where buildings and monuments from the Venetian era are distinctive.

The population of the country stands at just under 2 million and is almost exclusively Slovenian, which explains why the country had a relatively trouble-free divorce from Yugoslavia. With no substantial Serb minority to defend, Belgrade decided to let Slovenia go. There are, however, minority groups of Italians, predominantly along the coast, and Hungarians, mainly in Pomurje in the northeast, both of whom are guaranteed two seats in parliament. Slovenia's 7,000 Roma are also concentrated in the region of Pomurje.

During the Tito era, Slovenia received many thousand economic migrants from the poorer republics of Yugoslavia, and with the war of the 1990s, it also saw an influx of refugees. Some stayed and became integrated into society, some have returned to their homelands, and some remained in Slovenia but were never granted Slovenian nationality, leaving them stateless. The vast majority of Slovenes are Roman Catholics, while the Serbian Orthodox and Muslim faiths are represented in small numbers by migrants from the other countries of former Yugoslavia. There is a Serbian Orthodox church in Ljubljana, but plans to build a mosque in the capital have been repeatedly thwarted.

Historically, inland Slovenia, which was governed by the Habsburgs, used German as the official language, while the coast, which was under Venice, used Italian. Still today, local dialects borrow from German in the inland regions, and from Italian near the sea. When travelling along the coast, note that most towns and villages have two names, one Slovenian and one Italian, so that Koper is also known as Capodistria, and Portorož as Portorose.

Optimistic Outlook

In 2001 Slovenia was chosen to host the first summit between US President George W. Bush and Russian President Vladimir Putin, reflecting the excellent relationship between it and both other countries.

European pride

Slovenes are proud to be European, are better-informed about the EU than people of any other member country, and an above average number say they have benefited from membership. Recently questions have emerged on such issues as the effect of the EU on agriculture. Nine out of 10 Slovenes speak at least one foreign language.

The market on Shoemaker's Bridge in Ljubljana

Having joined the European Union (EU) in May 2004, Slovenia is currently living a period of economic growth and optimism. In fact, it had always been the most prosperous republic within former Yugoslavia, and politically also the most liberal. By 2006 the national economy was on a par with that of Greece and stronger than that of Portugal, and in January 2007, Slovenia became the first of the new EU member countries to adopt the Euro. Economic growth has slowed with tougher economic conditions around the world since 2008, and with pressure on Slovenian manufacturing from cheaper parts of the world. Questions such as taxation levels and the provision of state pensions have become major political issues.

Tourism is an important part of the Slovenian economy and has been growing steadily over recent years. Vast sums have been invested in upgrading hotels, developing spas and extending motorways, while tourism is diversifying into novelties such as weddings and night-time sledging trips. The boldest bid to attract tourists is a plan to create an artificial island on the Adriatic. If the project goes ahead, building will be complete by 2020. The island will be 30,000 sq metres (36,000 sq yds) in area and have beaches, restaurants and a marina.

A BRIEF HISTORY

Slovenia may be a small country, but its history is remarkably complex. Perched on the edge of the Balkan peninsula, through the centuries it has been repeatedly occupied, threatened and manipulated by outside forces, a feature which has only served to strengthen Slovenes' proud national identity and enrich the country's cultural repertoire.

Illyrians and Romans

The earliest known inhabitants of this region were called Illyrians by the Greeks. The most important archaeological find attributed to them is the 5th-century BC Vače situla, an ornately embossed bronze urn decorated with figures of men, women and animals, which was probably used for ritual drinking and is now on display in the National Museum in Ljubljana. In the 3rd century BC Celtic tribes arrived, and they too knew how to work metals.

In the 1st century BC the Romans began advancing towards the region, and by the 1st century AD they had conquered the Illyrian and Celtic tribes, and founded the inland garrison towns of Emona (Ljubljana), Poetovio (Ptuj) and Celeia (Celje). Developments within the Roman Empire were to have far-reaching repercussions for the Balkans: after the empire was split in AD395, the fault line between the Western Church of Rome

Vače situla, an ornate bronze urn, is the finest Illyrian artefact

Roman necropolis at Šempeter

and the Eastern Church of Byzantium ran through the region. In the east the Orthodox sects emerged (Serbs, Montenegrins and Macedonians), while Christians in the west were Roman Catholics (Slovenes and Croats).

The Western Roman Empire collapsed in the mid-5th century, and the region was stormed by Attila the Hun. The inhabitants of Emona, Poetovio and Celeia fled the Huns and founded Capris (Koper) and Piranum (Piran) on the Adriatic.

Early Slav States

The first Slav settlers arrived in the region during the 6th century, probably migrating from the Carpathian Basin. They settled in the river valleys, lived from farming, were superstitious and worshipped their own gods. In the 7th century they founded the Duchy of Karantania, the first Slavic state, with its centre close to Klagenfurt in present-day Austria. However, this was short-lived, as in 748 Karantania was incorporated into the Frankish Empire as Carinthia, converting to Christianity.

Over the following centuries the Slav people were reduced to serfdom by their overlords, though an independent kingdom under Carinthian Prince Loceij briefly appeared in 869–74 at the time the Frankish Empire was starting to break up.

In 900 the Magyars invaded the region before being driven back by the Germans, who divided Slovenian lands among their nobility and the Church. Between the 10th and 13th centuries many monasteries were built, as well as castles that would secure the borders against further attack.

The Habsburgs, Venice and the Ottoman Turks

The Habsburgs (whose family seat was originally in modern Switzerland) took control of inland Slovenia in 1335, dividing it into the Austrian crown lands of Carinthia, Carniola and Styria, and the royal family remained in power until 1918. During these six centuries, the upper classes were almost exclusively German, and the Slovenian language and culture was suppressed. In spite of the failure of repeated and determined revolts, the peasantry maintained their Slavic language and culture. Part of this was through the Reformation. Though the movement had little lasting effect on the region, books were published in Slovenian for the first time.

The Habsburg power did not extend to the coast, where towns came under the protection of the Venetian Empire, where they remained until the French arrived in 1797. This accounts for the distinctly Italianate buildings, dialect and cuisine of the ports and fishing villages.

After 1453, when Byzantium fell to Mehmet II, both the Habsburgs and the Venetians became preoccupied by the Ottoman Turks, who swept on through the Balkans

The lion of St Mark, symbol of Venice, on a door in Koper

towards Central Europe. Entire towns were fortified, and many hilltop castles reconstructed in an attempt to protect Slovenia against attack. To fund such projects, hefty taxes were imposed on the local population, which led to further unrest and revolt.

The economic and social situation improved during the relative peace of the 18th century and the reforms under Empress Maria Theresa. Small industries were founded, and road links improved between Trieste and Vienna. Compulsory primary-school education (albeit in German) was introduced and serfdom abolished. This prosperous period was celebrated in the ornate Baroque style that characterises several Slovenian cities, notably Ljubljana.

France Prešeren

France Prešeren was born into a farming family in Vrba, near Lake Bled, in 1800. He studied law in Vienna, then worked as a lawyer's assistant in Ljubljana. A vain and melancholy alcoholic and womaniser, Prešeren led a sad life full of disappointments. In 1835, following the death of a close friend, Matija Čop, and the realisation that his love for a local heiress, Julija Primič, would never be requited, he became suicidal.

From this time on, he wrote emotional romantic poems about unfulfilled love, the joys of drinking, and the beauty of his land and its women. He published only one volume of poetry, *Poezije*, in 1848, and his poems reached the public primarily through magazines. His work was unpopular with the Habsburgs due to its blatant anti-German sentiments, and was disapproved of by the Church, which considered his writing and lifestyle immoral. However, more than anyone else, he brought the idea of a Slovenian national identity to the people.

In 1846, he moved to Kranj where his house may be visited *(see page 37)*. He died of cirrhosis of the liver on 8 February 1849, now celebrated as Prešeren Day, a national holiday.

The Illyrian Provinces

In 1797 Napoleon conquered the Venetian Empire and a dozen years later succeeded in cutting Vienna off from the coast by taking Slovenia into his so-called Illyrian Provinces, extending from Graz in Austria all the way down the Eastern Adriatic to include Dalmatia.

Statue of the national poet France Prešeren in Ljubljana

Napoleon found favour among the Slovenes by making Ljubljana the capital of the Illyrian Provinces, and by allowing them to use Slovenian, rather then German, as the official language in schools and administration. This period of French rule also gave birth to the dream of a southern Slav state, which would unite Croats, Serbs and Slovenes, all of whom were represented in the Illyrian Provinces. But when Napoleon's defeat in Moscow in 1813 presaged the end of his empire two years later, Slovenia fell once again to Vienna.

Dreams of Independence

Once back in power, the Habsburgs set about suppressing Slovenian national aspirations and reinstalling the feudal system. But Slovenian pride and the dream of independence had taken root. It became the theme of the romantic poet France Prešeren (1800–49), author of *Zdravljica* (*A Toast*, 1844), which was chosen as the Slovenian national anthem when the country finally gained full independence in 1991. In 1848 Slovenian intellectuals founded the Zedinjena Slovenija (United Slovenia) movement, whose aim was to unify the Slovenian people and gain recognition of the Slovenian language. It did not succeed, but it inspired later movements.

Meanwhile, railways were arriving and industrialisation was taking place. Vienna was linked to Maribor in 1846, and a line extended through Ljubljana to Trieste in 1857.

World War and the Kingdom of Yugoslavia

When the Habsburg Archduke Franz Ferdinand was assassinated by a Serb nationalist in Sarajevo in 1914, Austria declared war on Serbia. Germany joined forces with Austria, while the Triple Entente (Russia, France and Britain) sided with Serbia, pulling Italy into the conflict by promising a portion of Slovenian territory as a reward. The result was the bloody fighting that took place along the River Soča (Isonzo in Italian), which was the Isonzo Front *(see box on page 46)*. Slovenes had the impossible choice of siding with the Habsburgs to keep their country intact, or opposing them and fighting fellow Slavs.

The defeat of the Austro-German alliance in 1918 saw the end of the Habsburg Empire. Inland Slovenia became part of the newly formed Kingdom of Serbs, Croats and Slovenes (in 1929 renamed the Kingdom of Yugoslavia, meaning Land of Southern Slavs) under Alexander I, while the Slovenian coast, as promised, was handed to Italy.

In 1941, Hitler declared war on the Kingdom of Yugoslavia. King Peter II left Belgrade for London, and the country was occupied by Axis forces, with Slovenia

Dual language: Tito Square in Slovenian and Italian

partitioned between Germany, Hungary and Italy. Josip Broz Tito, half-Slovene half-Croat by birth and leader of the Yugoslav Communist Party, set up the anti-fascist *Partizan* (Partisan) resistance movement, which succeeded in liberating the country in 1945.

Partisans on the entrance to the Parliament Building

With the war over and the monarchy gone, the Kingdom of Yugoslavia became the Socialist Federal Republic of Yugoslavia, made up of six republics including Slovenia, with Tito as President. Thousands of Slovenian and Croatian Nazi collaborators fled over the border to Austria, but British forces caught them in Bleiburg, disarmed them and sent them back to Yugoslavia, where many were executed.

Tito turned Yugoslavia into an extraordinary country. In 1948 he broke with the USSR, but he remained on amicable terms with both the communist East and capitalist West, gaining favours from both. Unlike the strict communism practised in the countries of the Eastern Bloc, Yugoslavian communism consisted of a market economy based on workers' self-management (co-operatives), and citizens were free to travel abroad, while foreigners could enter the country without visas. During the 1960s, the economy grew impressively, thanks to increased industrialisation and the beginnings of organised tourism. However, the gap between the richer and poorer republics also grew, and the coastal, tourist areas of Slovenia and Croatia objected to subsidising the poorer regions.

It was only Tito's remarkable charisma, and his belief in *Bratstvo i Jedinstvo* (Brotherhood and Unity) that held Yugoslavia together and kept nationalist aspirations at bay. Before his death in 1980, after 35 years in power, he attempted to prevent any one republic becoming too dominant by establishing a rotating presidency, so that each republic should take the helm for one year. But it was not to work.

Opposition and Independence

During the 1980s, hard-working Slovenia found itself producing 25 percent of Yugoslavia's export goods, despite making up only 8 percent of the population. With profits being siphoned by Belgrade, the Slovenes became increasingly frustrated. When, in 1988, the Yugoslavian People's Army (JNA) Military Council arrested and put on trial three journalists working for *Mladina*, a weekly satirical magazine, disenchantment and dissent increased still further, leading to the creation of an organised Slovenian opposition movement, which precipitated Slovenia's eventual secession from Yugoslavia.

Meanwhile in Serbia, Slobodan Milošević was fomenting a new wave of Serbian nationalism. In 1988, following riots by ethnic Albanians in Kosovo, he clamped down on the province by taking away its autonomy.

Lost citizens

In 1992 the names of 18,000 people who had been living in Slovenia without acquiring citizenship were removed from the registry of residents, losing their right to work, health and education. There are still as many as 6,000 without citizenship, and their case remains a controversial political issue.

This exhibition of power bode ill for tiny Slovenia, but the international community showed very little interest. With the fall of the Berlin Wall in 1989 marking the end of Eastern Bloc communism, Yugoslavia was no longer important to Western strategic interests.

Slovenian government building

Slovenia's first show of defiance against Belgrade came in January 1990, when Slovenian delegates, angered by Serbian and Montenegrin rejection of all of their proposals, walked out of the 14th Congress of the Yugoslav Communist Party. In April Slovenia held multi-party elections and a non-Communist government was formed, bringing with it calls for autonomy. Slovenia staged a referendum in December, in which 88 percent of the electorate voted for independence. Belgrade rejected Slovenia's request for secession.

Nevertheless, Slovenia declared independence on 25 June 1991, the same day as neighbouring Croatia, where Serbs formed a substantial minority. The following day, the JNA began moving towards the border, where it was met by Slovenian territorial defence units that had been stockpiling and importing arms.

But as the population was almost exclusively Slovenian, after the 'Ten-Day War' in which about 75 people died, Milošević had a change of mind and the JNA retreated back into Croatia. Independence was assured, and in May 1992 Slovenia was admitted to the United Nations.

Continuing Prosperity

Following independence, the country's economy initially went into decline, as Slovenia had lost its natural trading partners – the other former Yugoslav republics, several of which were at war – and gained an influx of refugees. Nevertheless, the country managed to return to prosperity, and the electorate strongly endorsed the centre-left government's application to join the European Union with an 89.6 percent 'yes' vote in a referendum in March 2003. Membership meant an injection of funds and other help, and by 2004 the economy picked up so much that when Slovenia entered the EU on 1 May it had the healthiest economy of all the 10 new members.

In October 2004 a new centre-right government pledged to accelerate privatisation, increase foreign direct investment (FDI) and lower taxes. By 2006, Slovenia had a GDP per capita on a level with Greece and ahead of Portugal.

Slovenia was the first new member country to fulfil the EU's Maastricht criteria for inflation and adopted the Euro on 1 January 2007. It was also the first new member state to hold the Presidency of the Council of the European Union, in 2008.

The economy has been affected by the global economic slow-down since 2008 and also by competition from developing countries, but is still growing.

Hot air balloons over Lake Ptuj

Historical Landmarks

1st century BC Romans arrive.
6th century AD Slavs arrive.
8th century AD Region comes under Franks. Slovenes begin converting to Christianity.
9th century Region passes to Dukes of Bavaria.
13th century Coastal towns take Venetian protectorate.
1335 Habsburgs take inland Slovenia.
15th and 16th centuries Ottoman Turks advance into the Balkans. Hilltop castles are built for defence. Succession of peasant uprisings.
1797 Fall of Venetian Empire. Coastal towns pass to Habsburgs.
1809 Slovenia absorbed into Napoleon's Illyrian Provinces with Ljubljana as capital.
1814 Fall of Napoleon. Slovenia back under Habsburg control.
1918 Fall of Austro-Hungary. Inland Slovenia becomes part of Kingdom of Serbs, Croats and Slovenes. Coast passes to Italy.
1941 Hitler declares war on Yugoslavia. Slovenia occupied by Axis forces.
1945 Tito founds Socialist Federal Republic of Yugoslavia, with Slovenia as one of six constituent republics.
1980 Tito dies, leaving Yugoslavia with rotating presidency.
1980s Economic crisis. Slovenia and Croatia object to funding poorer republics. Milošević in power in Belgrade as Serbian nationalism grows.
1989 Fall of Berlin Wall marks breakdown of Eastern Bloc and demise of communist ideals in Europe.
1990 Non-Communist government elected.
1991 Slovenia proclaims independence. 'Ten-Day War' ensues.
1992 EU and UN recognise Slovenia.
1993 Slovenia becomes member of IMF and World Bank.
2004 Slovenia joins EU along with nine other countries.
2007 Slovenia adopts the Euro.
2010 A referendum sends the Bay of Piran border dispute with Croatia to an international tribunal.
2011 Government collapses amid allegations of economic incompetence.

WHERE TO GO

Slovenia is small and compact, but incredibly diverse. From the central location of the capital, Ljubljana, almost anywhere can be reached in less than two hours. If you do not have a car, efficient buses link the capital to the most remote regions.

First-time visitors should start in Ljubljana, then explore the sublime mountains and lakes of the northwest, and round off with the splendid Venetian coastal towns of the southwest. The main draws of the northwest are the majestic alpine landscape of Triglav National Park and the emerald-green River Soča. The southwest is known for its 'coast and karst': the Italianate sea towns of Koper and Piran, the commercial resort of Portorož, plus the mysterious caves of Postojna and Škocjan, and Lipica Stud Farm. Less visited by foreigners but dear to many Slovenes, the southeast's architectural treasures include the monasteries and castles of Krka Valley, plus several spas. The flatter landscape of the northeast leads to the border with Hungary and the old Baroque towns of Maribor, Ptuj and Celje; there are also sophisticated thermal spas and a network of wine roads with cellars open to the public.

LJUBLJANA

Compact, easy-going and friendly, **Ljubljana** is a remarkably human city. The River Ljubljanica, crossed by elegant bridges and lined with weeping willows and open-air cafés, flows through the heart of the Old Town, lending an air of informality to the cobbled streets and Baroque buildings, while the whole scene is presided over by a proud hilltop castle. The city was founded in the 1st century BC by the Romans, ◀1

View of Ljubljana's rooftops from the castle

The rose-red Franciscan Church by the River Ljubljanica

who built a fortified military encampment, named Emona, on the left bank of the river, which was destroyed by the Huns in the mid-5th century AD. Slavs founded a second settlement on the right bank below the castle hill in the area that is now Old Square (Stari trg) and Town Square (Mestni trg), the heart of the city in the Middle Ages. This was largely destroyed by an earthquake in 1511, and rebuilt in Baroque style. After another earthquake, in 1895, new buildings took the Secessionist style, the Viennese Art Nouveau.

In the 1980s, Ljubljana was Yugoslavia's centre of underground culture, with punk rock bands and satirical magazines. Today's alternative scene lives on through the thriving student community, a large chunk of the city's 280,000 population.

Around Prešeren Square

Lying at the heart of the city is **Prešernov trg** (Prešeren Square), giving onto the Ljubljanica. Watched over by a bronze statue of poet France Prešeren (1800–49; *see box on page 18*), this square has a couple of notable Secessionist buildings, the **Urbanc** occupied by Centromerkur, Ljubljana's oldest department store, and the **Hauptman House** (Hauptmanova hiša). To the left is a small relief of Julija, Prešeren's lifelong love. City-dwellers meet on the steps that lead up the rose-and-cream façade of the 17th-century Baroque **Franciscan Church** (Frančiškanska cerkev).

Miklošičeva, the thoroughfare to the right of the church, is lined with Secessionist buildings, notably the white **Grand Hotel Union** by Josip Vancaš (1905) and the elegant former **Cooperative Bank** by Ivan and Helena Vurnik (1922; *pictured on page 12*), with colourful geometric patterns. Miklošičeva leads north to the train and bus stations.

From Prešeren Square the splendid white, three-span **Triple Bridge** (Tromostovje) by Jože Plečnik connects the city centre to the Old Town and gives visitors their first taste of the ingenious works of the famous architect. A

Jože Plečnik

Born in Ljubljana in 1872, Plečnik studied architecture in Vienna under the great early Modernist Otto Wagner, moving in 1911 to Prague where he supervised the renovation of Hradčany Castle and lectured at the School of Arts and Crafts. He returned to Ljubljana in 1921, became head of the university's new Faculty of Architecture, and set about transforming the face of the city, adding the Triple Bridge, the Shoemaker's Bridge, the National and University Library, Križanke Summer Theatre, Trnovo Bridge, the Central Market, Žale Cemetery and the Church of St Michael on the Marshes, all in a curious blend of Classical and Art Deco. **Plečnik House**, (Plečnikova hiša), his charming former home and studio, is at Karunova 4, in the eastern suburb of Trnovo (Tue–Thur 10am–2pm and 4pm–6pm, Sat 10am–2pm; charge; www.aml.si).

Dragon Bridge – the dragons are said to wag their tails

The Old Town

Though largely Baroque, the Old Town dates back to medieval times and is the only part of the city to have survived the 1895 earthquake. To the right of the Triple Bridge, the waterside promenade of **Cankarjevo nabrežje** is lined with cafés, and holds the Sunday morning **flea market**, with stalls selling antiques and bric-a-brac, including memorabilia of Communist Yugoslavia.

Left of the Triple Bridge lies the **Central Market** (Glavna tržnica), an open-sided colonnade designed by Plečnik in 1939. It runs upstream all the way to the Art Nouveau **Dragon Bridge** (Zmajski most). The green dragons at its four corners are said to wag their tails each time a virgin crosses the bridge. Inside the Central Market, the lower level beside the water has fishmongers' stalls, while the upper level accommodates a variety of stalls. The landward side opens onto **Vodnikov trg** (Vodnik Square), where a colourful market is held (Mon–Sat, most stalls around 7am–2pm), with stallholders selling seasonal fruit and vegetables, fresh flowers, honey, beeswax candles, dried herbs and clothes.

West of Vodnik Square stands the 18th-century Baroque **Cathedral of St Nicholas** (Stolna cerkev svetega Nikolaja), designed by Italian architect and Jesuit monk Andrea Pozzo. Close to the river, it is aptly dedicated to St Nicholas, the protector of sailors and fishermen. The modern bronze doors commemorate Pope John Paul II's visit in 1996.

Between Vodnik Square and the castle hill, at **Krekov trg** (Krek Square) 10, lies the **Ljubljana City Tourist Board** (tel: 01-306 12 15; www.visitljubljana.si). Check out cultural events, book places on guided city tours or hire a bicycle here.

Close by lies **Mestni trg** (Town Square), a cobbled square overlooked by the 18th-century **Town Hall** (Rotovž). The charming Baroque **Robba Fountain** (Robbov vodnjak), a three-sided obelisk, was designed by the Italian Francesco Robba in 1751 to represent Slovenia's three rivers, the Ljubljanica, Sava and Krka. Mestni trg leads to **Stari trg** (Old Square), with elegant pastel-coloured Baroque buildings housing lively cafés, boutiques and galleries, and becomes **Gornji trg** (Upper Square). B

The castle walls and observation tower

The Castle

A signed path to the left of Gornji trg leads through woodland to the top of the castle hill, which is crowned by **Ljubljana Castle** (Ljubljanski grad; daily summer 9am–10pm, winter 10am–9pm). Many other paths lead to the castle, and a funicular railway runs from Krekov trg (daily every 10 minutes, same hours as castle; charge). Although there has been a fortress here since medieval times, the castle that you see today is the result of reconstruction following the 1511 earthquake. Through the

French café on French Revolution Square

centuries, the castle has been occupied by provincial leaders, and has been used as a garrison, a prison and a home for the poor. The glass, steel and concrete restaurant in the central courtyard was installed as part of renovations in the 1980s. From June to mid-September the castle is one of several venues for the Ljubljana Summer Festival (www.ljubljanafestival.si). However, the highlight is a climb to the top of the 150-step, 19th-century **Observation Tower** (summer 9am–9pm, winter 10am–6pm), where there are stunning views over the city's terracotta rooftops to the Julian Alps. Below the tower, the **Virtual Museum** (hours same as the tower; charge) gives a 20-minute multimedia presentation of the city's history.

The Centre

The second bridge downstream from the Triple Bridge is Plečnik's pedestrian **Shoemaker's Bridge** (Čevljarski most), which leads back to the modern city centre, a district of shops, offices and government buildings interspersed with a number of squares and museums. A short distance southwest of the bridge lies **Trg francoske revolucije** (French Revolution Square), which commemorates the years when Ljubljana was the capital of Napoleon's Illyrian Provinces (1809–13). On the south side, **Križanke Summer Theatre** (Križanke poletno gledališče) is a former monastery belonging to the Knights of the Cross, converted into an open-air theatre by Plečnik and now a Summer Festival venue.

Just east of Križanke, at Gosposka 15, the **City Museum** (Mestni muzej; Tue–Sun 10am–6pm; charge; www.mgml.si) offers an entertaining audio-visual presentation of Ljubljana's history, and also has a pleasant café.

North of Križanke, on Turjaška, is the **National and University Library** (Narodna i univerzitetna knjižnica or NUK; members only), built in 1941 with a façade of rough grey stone and orange brick, and massive copper doors with horse-head handles. Many consider it Plečnik's greatest work. To the north is **Kongresni trg** (Congress Square), known as Star (Zvezda), a large green patch laid out for the Congress of the Holy Alliance in 1821 and overlooked by the **Philharmonic Hall** (Slovenska filharmonija; *see page 95*) from 1892.

East of Kongresni trg lies the less appealing **Trg republike** (Republic Square), and the colossal 1970s concrete Cankarjev Dom *(see pages 95–6)*, a multi-purpose cultural centre. Here, too, is the 1959 **Parliament Building**, with a two-storey portal stacked with statues of workers by Zdenko Kalin and Karl Putrih.

West of the busy thoroughfare of Slovenska lies the main conglomeration of museums. At Prešernova 24 the **National Gallery** (Narodna galerija; Tue–Sun 10am–6pm; charge; www.

The neo-Renaissance National Museum has archaeological finds

ng-slo.si) has Slovenian and European paintings from the Baroque period to the late 19th century. Close by, at Cankarjeva 15, the recently renovated **Museum of Modern Art** (Moderna galerija; Tue–Sun 10am–6pm; charge; www.mg-lj.si) has Slovenian 20th-century painting and sculpture, and also hosts the International Biennial of Graphic Arts in odd-numbered years. A few doors away at Prešernova 20, the **National Museum** (Narodni muzej; Fri–Wed 10am–6pm, Thur 10am–8pm; charge; www.narmuz-lj.si) is filled with archaeological finds, most notably the Vače situla *(see page 15)*. The building also houses the **Natural History Museum**.

Tivoli Park and Beyond

For a stroll amid rolling parkland, cross the busy Tivolska (there is a subway near the Museum of Modern Art) to reach **Tivoli Park**, the city's major recreation area. An elegant white Baroque building contains the **International Centre of Graphic Arts** (Mednarodni grafični likovni center; Wed–Sun 10am–6pm; charge; www.mglc-lj.si), housing a collection of fine art prints from the 20th century up until today.

If you are travelling with children you might consider the **Atlantis Water Park**, (daily 9am–11pm; charge; www.atlantis-vodnomesto.si), situated 3km (2 miles) northeast of the city centre in **BTC City**, a vast shopping and entertainment complex.

Tivoli Park

NORTHWEST

With snowcapped alpine mountains, dense pine forests, emerald meadows and two beautiful lakes, this region is an undoubted highlight of Slovenia. From Ljubljana the first stop is lakeside Bled, the country's most visited resort. From here the landscape becomes increasingly mountainous, with an average altitude of over 2,000m (6,500ft), taking in Triglav National Park and Kranjska Gora ski resort, before mellowing into Soča Valley's woodland, gorges and turquoise river.

Škofja Loka

From Ljubljana, on the A2 northwest to Bled, there is a
2 a popular detour to **Škofja Loka** on the River Sora 19km (12 miles) from the city. During the Middle Ages this delightful town was a regional centre for craftsmen and their guilds. Fortified in the 14th century, it was largely destroyed in an earthquake in 1511, and most of the painted façades and elegant churches date from 16th-century reconstruction.

Local treat

Above: a quiet street in Škofja Loka. Look out for the local speciality, *kruhek*, decorated unleavened bread made with honey and cinnamon and shaped in wooden moulds. You will find these tasty treats for sale in several shops around town.

The old town centres on the **Mestni trg** (Town Square), the medieval marketplace, overlooked by the imposing **Town Hall** (Rotovž) and **Homan House** (Homan hiša), both of which mix Baroque and Gothic elements and are decorated externally with 16th-century frescos. West of Mestni trg, the hilltop **castle** (grad), rebuilt in the 16th century after an earthquake, houses the **Loka Museum** (Loški muzej; Mon 10am–2pm, Tue–Sun 10am–6pm; charge; www.loski-muzej.si), with an interesting ethnographic section giving some idea of the lives of local peasants in feudal times.

The town is known throughout Slovenia for the Škofja Loka Passion (Škofjeloški pasijon), a Passion play written in 1721, the oldest dramatic text in the Slovenian language. Performances were revived during the 1990s. There are no fixed dates, but if it's taking place you can't miss it, with 600 actors participating in 20 scenes, and four stages around town. Also, on the last weekend in June, a medieval street fair called the Venus Journey (Venerina pot) takes place, with local craftsmen demonstrating pottery, lacemaking and basketry on Mestni trg, plus street entertainers including fire eaters and swordsmen.

Loka's 16th-century castle

The undulating green hills west of town are a haven for hiking and biking. Bicycles can be rented from **Škofja Loka Tourist Information Centre** at Mestni trg 7, and they can also supply a map of the 30km (19-mile) Loka bike trail, leading through the surrounding villages.

Kranj

Located at the confluence of rivers Sava and Kokra, 10km (6 miles) north of Škofja Loka (or 25km northwest of Ljubljana if you keep to the A2), **Kranj** is Slovenia's fourth-largest town. Its uninspiring industrial suburbs belie a pleasant old town, at the heart of which is the **Main Square** (Glavni trg), rimmed by Gothic and Renaissance buildings. Nearby, at Prešernova 7, is the late-Gothic **Prešeren House** (Prešernova hiša; Tue–Sun 10am–6pm; charge), former home of Slovenia's best-known poet, France Prešeren *(see page 18)*

A quiet corner of Kranj, Slovenia's fourth-largest town

The ground floor is devoted to temporary exhibitions, while on the first floor you can see his bedroom and office (he was a lawyer as well as a romantic poet), complete with early 19th-century furniture, plus a memorial museum displaying manuscripts, including translations of his works into Bengali and Chinese.

Tucked away in a narrow valley below the slopes of Jelovica, 11km (7 miles) northwest of Kranj, lies **Kropa**. This mining village has a long history of wrought-iron making. The **Iron Forging Museum** (Kovaški muzej; Jan–Feb Tue–Fri 8am–3pm, Mar–Apr Nov–Dec, Tue, Thur, Fri 8am–3pm, Wed, Sat, Sun 10am–12pm 3pm–5pm, May–Oct Tue–Sun 10am–6pm; charge; www.muzeji-radovljica.si) traces the development of iron working from the 15th century to its 19th century decline, and the rise of handmade nails in the 20th century. There is a section dedicated to the work of local master smith Joža Bertoncelj.

Radovljica

A sleepy provincial town, **Radovljica** is 21km (13 miles) northwest of Kranj. Honey making has been an important branch of agriculture in Slovenia since the 18th century, and Radovljica's unusual **Beekeeping Museum** (Čebelarski muzej; Jan–Feb Tue–Fri 8am–3pm, Mar–Apr Nov–Dec, Tue, Thur, Fri 8am–3pm, Wed, Sat, Sun 10am–12pm 3pm–5pm, May–Oct Tue–Sun 10am–6pm; charge; www.muzeji-radovljica.si) in a Baroque manor house on the main square at Linhartov trg 1, tells the story of beekeeping and the indigenous Grey Carniolan bee. Painted wooden beehive panels are a local folk art, intended to enable each beekeeper to identify his hives. Some depict scenes from the Bible and others capture amusing moments from everyday rural life. Next door to the Beekeeping Museum, Gostilna Lectar *(see page 110)* is a highly regarded restaurant, perfect for sampling traditional Slovenian dishes.

Lake Bled

Within a basin surrounded by the rugged, snowcapped Ju-
3 lian Alps lies **Bled**, Slovenia's most visited resort, 50km (30 miles) northwest of Ljubljana. The jewel of this idyllic hideaway is the emerald-green Lake Bled, inset with a small island and church and guarded by a clifftop castle.

Tourism began here in 1855, when European aristocrats began visiting the lake to enjoy its efficacious thermal waters and the invigorating alpine air. Today, busloads of excursionists come from all over Europe, but the lake and its setting remain undeniably beautiful. Hotels and guesthouses cater for every budget, and there are bathing facilities, and boats and bicycles to rent. Wedding ceremonies in the castle are the most recent diversification in the tourist market.

Though a popular spot, few people venture far from town, and it's easy to escape the crowds by walking the 6km (4-

mile) perimeter of the lake along a waterside path lined with lime trees, horse chestnuts and weeping willows.

The most impressive views of the lake are from the ramparts of **Bled Castle** (Blejski grad; daily Apr–Oct 8am–8pm; Nov–Mar 8am–6pm; charge; www.blejski-grad.si), built on a rocky outcrop 100m (330ft) above the water. Dating from the 11th century, its present appearance is largely 17th-century. Inside is the **Castle Museum** (Grajski muzej), with archaeological finds, period furniture and armoury. 4

In the middle of the western half of the lake is **Bled Island** (Blejski otok), where an elegant church and belltower poke through the trees. To visit it, either rent a rowing boat or take a guided trip on a *pletnja* (like a Venetian gondola) from the landing station opposite Vila Prešeren close to the centre of town. A continuous flight of 99 steps lead from the island's quay up to the 17th-century Baroque **Church**

Lake Bled with Bled Island, reached by rowing boat or *pletnja*

of the Assumption, a popular place for weddings because the early Slavs built a pagan temple to Živa, their goddess of love and fertility, on the site. The highlight of the ceremony is a challenge for the groom to carry his bride up all 99 steps without stopping. The adjoining 15th-century bell tower is said to bring good luck to those who ring the bell.

On the north bank of the lake, directly below the castle, lie the **Castle Swimming Grounds** (Grajsko kopališče; mid-June–late Sept daily 8am–7pm; charge), while on the west side of the lake, the Rowing Centre (Veslaški center) organises the Bled International Regatta each year in mid-June, attracting world-class oarsmen. Nearby, the free public bathing area with lawns running down to the water is a pleasant place to swim and sunbathe.

On the south bank, a 20-minute walk from town, set in manicured gardens, **Vila Bled** *(see page 138)* was largely built by the Yugoslav royal family in the early 20th century as a summer mansion. Tito used it as a retreat and to entertain world leaders, including Indira Ghandi and Nikita Krushchev. Since 1984 it has been a luxury hotel.

Golf & Country Club Bled, 3km (2 miles) east of Bled, is considered one of the most beautiful in Europe *(see page 89)*.

Old-Fashioned Steam Train

Throughout the summer, an old-fashioned steam locomotive runs from Jesenice (12km/8miles north of Bled), past the lakes of Bled and Bohinj. It stops at Bled and Bohinjska Bistrica stations, then passes through the 6.3km (4-mile) Bohinj Tunnel under the 1,277m (4,190ft) mountain of Bohinjsko Sedlo, emerging in the village of Podbrdo to enter the narrow, steep-sided Bača Valley and eventually arrive in Most na Soči close to the Italian border. For more information, visit the Slovenian Railways website, www.slo-zeleznice.si.

Triglav National Park

Vintgar Gorge

The spectacular **Vintgar Gorge** (Blejski vintgar; daily May– 5
Oct sunrise–sunset; charge) lies 4km (2½ miles) north of Bled. Carved by the River Radovna and flanked by rocky outcrops and birch woods, it was first explored in 1891. A series of suspended wooden walkways and bridges criss-cross the length of the 1,600m (1-mile) gorge, passing over thundering waterfalls and rapids and culminating with the 13m (43ft) high Šum Waterfall (Slap Šum).

Triglav National Park

Triglav National Park attracts 2.5 million visitors a year. Its stunning alpine mountains, valleys, lakes and rivers offer a dramatic backdrop to outdoor activities such as hiking and cycling and white-water rafting, plus skiing in winter. There are 25 settlements in the park and a population of 2,200. Protected animals include brown bears, lynx and golden eagles.

Wild and unspoilt Lake Bohinj in Triglav National Park

Lake Bohinj

While Lake Bled is postcard-perfect, its sister lake 26km (16 miles) southwest in Triglav National Park is larger and wilder, set in unspoilt alpine landscape of pine woods and lush meadows speckled with wild flowers, against a backdrop of snow-capped mountains. 6 Unlike Bled, **Lake Bohinj** (Bohinjsko Jezero) is almost untouched by modern development; building on the shores of the lake is prohibited. Bohinj is an excellent base for hiking, with a number of well-kept mountain paths.

At **Ribčev Laz**, a small tourist settlement on the east bank, you can find Hotel Jezero *(see page 138)*, a Tourist Information Centre (at No. 48) stocking local hiking maps, and several agencies catering for adventure sports and hiring bicycles, kayaks and canoes *(see page 85)*. It is also possible to swim near here; the best places lie along the northeast corner of the lake. Alternatively, keen walkers may embark on a 12km (8-mile) hike around the perimeter of the lake.

Ribčev Laz also has the elegant whitewashed medieval **Church of St John the Baptist** (Cerkev svetega Janeza), decorated with 15th- and 16th-century biblical frescos on the inside and a large St Christopher outside by the door.

From the small quay opposite the church, regular boats (May–Oct 10am–5.30pm, departures every 90min; journey time 30min) shuttle visitors from Ribčev Laz to Camp Zlatorog in the small holiday village of **Ukanc** at the west end of the lake. Alternatively, the road along the south shore also leads to Ukanc, 4.5km (2½ miles) away. From here, a marked footpath heads west to the popular **Savica Waterfall** (Slap Savica; Apr–Oct 8am–6pm; charge), a 97m (318ft) cascade of water thundering into a deep gorge, which is reached by a steep set of steps. The most popular hiking route up **Mount Triglav**, Slovenia's highest mountain (2,864m/9,396ft), begins in Ukanc.

South of Ukanc, the **Vogel cable-car** (daily every half hour, 7
summer 7am–6pm, winter 8am–6pm; charge) takes visitors up to the **Vogel Ski Centre**, at an altitude of 1,535m (5,036ft). From here, the view of the lake and the surrounding mountains is superb.

Mount Triglav

With its distinctive three peaks (Triglav means 'three heads'), Triglav enchanted the early Slavs, who believed it to be the home of a three-headed god who ruled the sky, the earth and the underworld. Today it is the symbol of Slovenia, and is featured on the country's flag. National pride decrees that every true Slovene should reach the 2,864m (9,396ft) peak of the mountain at least once in their lifetime, and there is an annual climb of '100 Women on Mount Triglav' to highlight the role of women. The ascent can be very demanding and is usually broken by at least one overnight stay in a mountain hut.

Back at the east end of the lake, northeast of Ribčev Laz, a scattering of peaceful alpine farming villages offer rustic restaurants, rooms to let and a couple of small museums. In a 19th-century dairy in **Stara Fužina**, a short walk north of Ribčev Laz, the **Alpine Dairy Museum** (Planšarski muzej; Tue–Sun July–Aug 11am–7pm, Jan–June and Sept–Oct 10am–noon and 4–6pm; charge) presents the history of dairy farming and cheese making in the area. In **Studor** (1.5km/1 mile east of Stara Fužina), the **Oplen House** (Oplenova hiša; opening times as Alpine Dairy Museum above; charge) is a typical 19th-century, stone-and-wood farmhouse, with a 'black kitchen' for smoking ham, a loom for weaving and original farm tools. The well-signed **Mrcina Ranč** (www.ranc-mrcina.com) is a riding centre in Studor with Icelandic ponies for trekking.

Kranjska Gora to Trenta

Northwest of Bled, close to both the Austrian and Italian borders, lies **Kranjska Gora**, Slovenia's biggest and best-known skiing resort *(see page 86)* and also a good base for hiking in summer. Each year in March, Kranjska Gora hosts the Planica Ski Jumping World Cup Championship, and it was here that Finland's Matti Hautamaki jumped an amazing 231m (758ft) in 2003, a world record that held for two years. The resort is well equipped with big hotels and family-run guest houses, though there are few cultural attractions besides the **Liznjek House** (Liznjekova domačija; Tue–Sat 10am–6pm, Sun 10am–5pm; charge; www.gornjesavskimuzej.si), an 18th-century brick-and-wood farmhouse devoted to an ethnographic exhibition. The **Kranjska Gora Fun Bike Park** (May–mid-June, Sept–Oct Mon–Fri 9am–5pm, mid-Jun–Aug daily 9am–6pm; charge; www.bikepark.si) offers a series of exciting downhill tracks plus mountain bikes to rent.

Alpine landscape around Kranjska Gora

Between Kranjska Gora and Trenta, the spectacular **Vršič Pass** is a 25km (15-mile) stretch of hairpin bends commanding stunning views and rising to an altitude of 1,611m (5,285ft). The pass was built during World War I to enable supplies to reach the Austrian army fighting along the Soča Front *(see box on page 46)*. It is often blocked by heavy snow during winter. 8

The village of **Trenta**, 25km (15 miles) south of Kranjska Gora, is worth a stop to look in the **Triglav National Park Information Centre**, housed in the Trenta Lodge (daily May–Oct 10am–6pm, Jan–Apr 10am–2pm; www.soca-trenta.si), which has an informative multimedia presentation of the park's geology and indigenous flora and fauna. The centre also offers guided hiking tours following the 20km (12-mile) Soča Trail.

Close by, the **Julian Alps Botanical Garden** (Alpinum Juliana; May–Sept 8.30am–6.30pm; charge; www.soca-trenta.si)

specialises in high-altitude Alpine flora. Founded in 1925 by Albert Bois de Chesne, most of the plants it displays are indigenous to the region, though there is a small area reserved for non-endemic species from the French Pyrenees and Caucasus. The garden is at its most beautiful in May and the beginning of June.

Lepena Valley

Further southwest is the road junction for the **Lepena Valley** on the left between Trenta and Bovec. Here, on a green plateau overlooking the Soča Valley, you will find the idyllic **Pristava Lepena** *(see page 91)*, a low-key holiday village combining traditional wooden Alpine cottages, a riding centre with Lipizzaner horses for trekking, and a good restaurant.

Soča Valley

Bovec, 35km (22 miles) southwest of Kranjska Gora, marks the beginning of the rocky gorges and dense pine forests of the remote **Soča Valley**. The area is a popular destination for

The Soča Front

When Italy entered World War I in 1915, intending to advance east into Austro-Hungarian territory, the River Soča (Isonzo in Italian) became the natural front line, running some 90km (55 miles) south from Bovec almost to Trieste on the Adriatic coast. After 29 months of fighting, the decisive battle, the 'Miracle at Kobarid', took place in 1917, in which the combined forces of the Central Powers defeated the Italian army. Fighting in the Soča Valley resulted in the deaths of an estimated 1 million soldiers and civilians, plus a mass exodus of inhabitants from the area, very few of whom ever returned. Ernest Hemingway, who was working as a volunteer ambulance driver for the Italian forces, based his novel *A Farewell to Arms* on this experience.

adventure-sports enthusiasts, who enjoy kayaking, canoeing, rafting and canyoning on the turquoise **River Soča**, which flows south as far as Nova Gorica (after which it runs into Italy and becomes known as the Isonzo).

Bovec started out as a ski resort *(see page 86)*, but now caters for adventure sports from May to September. Due to a series of natural disasters including a fire and two earthquakes, plus the destruction of World War I, the town centre is modern and functional but offers no notable cultural attractions. However, 6km (4 miles) southwest of Bovec, the **Boka Waterfall** (Slap Boka), in two stages of 38m (125ft) and 106m (348ft), is impressive enough to warrant a stop.

Kayaking on the River Soča

Kobarid

The peaceful Alpine town of **Kobarid**, 21km (13 miles) south of Bovec, lies in the shadow of Mount Krn (2,244m/7,360ft). Its cultural attraction is **Kobarid Museum** (Kobariški muzej, Gregorčičeva 10; Apr–Sept Mon–Fri 9am–6pm, Sat–Sun 9am–7pm, Oct–Mar Mon–Fri 10am–5pm, Sat–Sun 9am–6pm; charge; www.kobariski-muzej.si) in the 18th-century Mašer House. This anti-war collection gives a thought-provoking account of the fighting that took place along the banks of the River Soča during World War I *(see* 9

Kobarid Museum remembers the front line in World War I

box on page 46). Exhibits include photos, maps, scale models, flags, military uniforms and arms. The museum runs the 5km (3-mile) **Kobarid Historic Walk** (Kobariška zgodovinska pot), and can provide a self-guiding pamphlet and map. This well-marked path crosses green meadows and a stone canyon to take in sites related to World War I, including the Italian front line where one can still make out the trenches, and the Italian War Memorial, a monumental octagonal mausoleum holding the bodies of more than 7,000 Italian soldiers killed during the fighting. It starts and finishes at **Trg svobode**, the main square.

Kobarid's other big pull for visitors is its river-based sports activities. There are a number of agencies based here that can arrange rafting, canyoning, kayaking and canoeing trips *(see page 85)* from May to September. Trout-fishing enthusiasts can pick up a permit from Hotel Hvala *(see page 139)* on the main square. The season runs from April to October.

Nova Gorica

Best known for its 24-hour casinos, **Nova Gorica**, 53km (33 miles) south of Kobarid, is a 'new town' on the border with Italy. After World War II, the predominantly Slovenian-speaking town of Gorizia was awarded to Italy. To compensate for the loss, Tito set about building a new town (Nova Gorica means New Gorizia) with the designs of Slovenian architect Edo Ravnikar. The result is the concrete apartment blocks and landscaped green parks of today.

Despite its interesting past, Nova Gorica is a dull place. The main attraction is its numerous casinos, popular with Italians who hop over the border in busloads daily. Slovenia's largest casino, and reputedly one of the biggest in Europe, occupies the ground floor of **Hotel Casino Perla** *(see page 139)*. Open all day every day, it has 48 gaming tables for roulette and blackjack, and 800 slot machines.

Dobrovo

The region of **Goriška Brda** is known for its undulating hills planted with vineyards and its fine cellars stocking red and white wines. Close to the Italian border, its largest settlement and chief wine-producing centre is **Dobrovo**, 16km (10 miles) northwest of Nova Gorica.

The town's main sight is the white 16th-century Renaissance **Dobrovo Castle** housing the **Dobrovo Castle Museum Collection** (Muzejska zbirka grad Dobrovo;

Unified piazza

For more than 40 years Nova Gorica and Gorizia were separated by tough border control. Everything changed on 30 April 2004, the day before Slovenia's entry into the EU, with celebrations in Piazza Transalpina to mark the start of free movement. Once divided by a wire mesh barrier, the piazza is now a symbol of European unification. A mosaic has been made including fragments of the numbers 57/15 that once marked the border stone in the centre of the square.

Tue–Fri 8am–4pm, Sat–Sun noon–4pm; charge). On the first floor, next to the Knights' Hall, the 19th-century cultural history collection is worth a look, as are the prints by local 20th-century artist Zoran Mušič on the second floor. However, most people come to the castle to visit **Vinoteka Brda**, (Tue–Sun, 11.30am–9pm; tel: 05-395 92 10; www.vinotekabrda.si), which offers wine tasting in a stone-vault cellar in the castle courtyard.

Close by at Zadružna cesta 9, the **Goriška Brda wine cellars** (May–Dec Mon–Fri 8am–7pm, Sat 8am–5pm, Jan–Apr Mon–Fri 8am–5pm, Sat 8am–1pm; tel: 05-331 01 00; www.klet-brda.com) make another fine venue for wine tasting, being the largest wine cellar in Slovenia, storing a staggering 18 million litres (4 million gallons) of wine.

SOUTHWEST: INLAND

The southwest is made up of two contrasting but complementary regions: the coast and the Karst region.

Slovenia has just 47km (30 miles) of seaboard, but it is well worth seeing for its delightful ports enriched with Venetian-style architecture, and for enjoying the country's most popular seaside resort, Portorož. The main draws of the inland Karst region, an attractive region of steep, cultivated valleys, are its extraordinary labyrinth of underground caves and the world-renowned Lipizzaner horses.

Idrija

From Ljubljana, the A1 leads southwest to Koper. En route, a possible detour is **Idrija**, 60km (38 miles) from the capital, in a valley at the confluence of the rivers Idrijca and Nikova. Mercury was discovered here in 1490, and when production reached its peak in the second half of the 18th century, Idrija was providing 13 percent of the world market. However, by the late 20th century mercury was regarded as a serious pollutant, capable of causing brain damage. The world price fell and the last mine closed in 1999. Tours of **Idrija Mercury Mine** (Antonijev rov; tours Mon–Fri 10am and 3pm, Sat–Sun 10am, 3pm and 4pm; charge; www.rzs-idrija.si) begin with an audio-visual presentation about the history of the town and the mine, after which visitors don helmets and jackets and are led on an atmospheric 1,200m (¾-mile) circular route through the mine and a unique 18th-century underground chapel.

The town is dominated by the 16th-century **Gewerkenegg Castle** (Grad Gewerkenegg), built as the mine's administrative centre, and now the **Town Museum** (Mestni muzej; Tue–Fri 9am–6pm; charge; www.muzej-idrija-cerkno.si), giving visitors an insight into the history of Idrija's mercury-mining industry. There is also a permanent gallery collection comprising of prints and paintings by renowned Slovene and Italian artists, as well as a section on the craft of lacemaking. A lace school was established in 1876, and Idrija is known throughout Slovenia for the craft, which is still alive today.

Each year in late June, Idrija hosts a 10-day Lacemaking Festival (Čipkarski

The clock tower of Idrija's Gewerkenegg Castle

festival) with displays and events all around the town. On **Mestni trg**, the main square, there are several small boutiques where you can buy lace all year round.

While you're in Idrija, call in at **Restauracija Barbara** (Mon–Fri 4pm–10pm; *see page 111*) to try the local speciality, *žlikrofi*, potato balls flavoured with marjoram and wrapped in pasta, similar to Italian ravioli.

Human fish

Below: the *Proteus anguinus*, known in Slovenia as the 'human fish', is a flesh-pink amphibian salamander endemic to the karst caves. Growing to about 25–30cm, it can live for up to a hundred years, many spent in total darkness. With no eyes but a keen sense of smell, it feeds on crustacea and worms, although its very slow metabolism allows it to survive for many years without eating at all.

The Karst Region

The dramatic Karst region is a wild, barren, rocky landscape interspersed with vineyards, pine woods and rural villages of grey limestone cottages. It lies between Postojna and the coast. The word *karst* (*kras* in Slovenian) originated here, and has since been adopted as the international term for the geological phenomenon characterised by sinkholes, underground streams and caves with stalactites and stalagmites, which occurs in limestone areas.

Postojna Cave

Europe's most visited cave, and probably your first choice for a cave tour, is near the town of **Postojna**, 44km (27 miles) southwest of

10 Ljubljana. **Postojna Cave** (Postojnska jama; tours daily May–Sept on the hour 9am–5pm, Apr and Oct 10am, noon, 2pm and 4pm, Nov–Mar 10am, noon and 3pm; charge; www.postojna-cave.com) comprises 20km (13 miles) of halls and passages, of which a quarter is open to the public. The 90-minute tour starts with a train ride through 3.5km (2 miles) of ingeniously lit tunnels and grottoes dripping with stalactites and stalagmites. The remaining 1.5km (1 mile) covered on foot takes in the stunning **Concert Hall**, which can hold audiences of up to 10,000 and is occasionally used for concerts. At Christmas it becomes a 'living crib' accompanied by carol singing.

Stalactites inside Postojna Cave

The **Speleobiological Station** close to the cave entrance shows a short film about the karst, and displays live specimens of cave fauna, including the bizarre 'human fish' inside an aquarium *(see box opposite)*. It is amazing to think that anything at all can live in these conditions.

Predjama Castle

The magically beautiful **Predjama Castle** (Predjamski Grad; daily July–Aug 9am–7pm, May, Jun and Sept 9am–6pm, Apr and Oct 10am–6pm, Nov–Mar 10am–4pm; charge; www.postojna-cave.com) lies near the village of Predjama 7km (4 11

Ice surfing on Lake Cerknica

miles) northwest of Postojna Cave. Built into the rocks of a sheer cliff face, it dates back to the 13th century, though its present Renaissance appearance is largely the result of 16th-century alterations. Inside, several rooms are furnished in period style, the stairs to the upper floors are carved in solid bedrock, and below the castle there's a **cave** (May–Sept variable hours, Oct–Apr closed due to bats).

Lake Cerknica

The 'disappearing' lake is another of the region's typical karst features. This unusual natural phenomenon is 8km (5 miles) east of Postojna. It vanishes completely in the summer, but from October to June it fills up with water, and is at its largest in spring, when it is approximately 10km (6 miles) long and 5km (3 miles) wide, but never deeper than 5m (16ft). Locals enjoy fishing and windsurfing here, and it's also a popular spot with birdwatchers.

Škocjan Caves

12 The **Škocjan Caves** (Škocjanske jame; tours June–Sept daily on the hour 10am–5pm, Nov–Mar Mon–Sat 10am and 1pm, Sun 10am, 1pm and 3pm, Apr–May daily 10am, 1pm and 3.30pm; charge; www.park-skocjanske-jame.si) are a Unesco World Heritage Site that attracts 90,000 visitors every year (sport footwear and a warm sweater are recommended). They lie 26km (16 miles) southwest of Postojna, and 5km (3 miles) southeast of Divača. The 90-minute tour of the caves takes visitors on foot through 2.5km (1½ miles) of the total 6km (4-mile) network.

The main sights are the **Silent Cave**, decorated with stalagmites and stalactites, and the unforgettable **Murmuring Cave**, an underground gorge some 300m long, 60m wide and 100m high (980 x 200 x 330ft), carved by the emerald-green River Reka which roars and echoes in the cave. It is crossed by the narrow Cerkvenik Bridge, which is suspended a hair-raising 45m (150ft) above the water. Close by, the **Škocjan Educational Trail** is a well-marked path running through the Škocjan Caves park, and introduces visitors to the surrounding natural and cultural features of the area.

Lipica Stud Farm

The peaceful green pastures and whitewashed stables of
13 the **Lipica Stud Farm** (Kobilarna Lipica; daily, tours on the hour, times vary, shorter hours and closed Monday in winter; charge; www.lipica.org) lie 7km (4 miles) south of Divača off the A1. The birthplace of the Lipizzaner white horses was

A pair of Lipizzaner horses

Lipizzaner horses

Lipizzaner horses are born black or brown and turn white around the age of seven. They stand 15–15.3hh (1.55–1.58m/61–2in), have long powerful backs and strong muscular necks, and can be trained to perform intricate dressage steps. Slovenia's entry to the Eurozone is marked by the Lipizzaner horse on the 20-cent coin.

founded in 1580 by the Habsburgs, who wanted to create an elegant cart- and saddle-horse for their court. They imported Berber horses from Spain, which had been brought to Europe by the Moors from North Africa, and crossed them with Arab horses and local Karst ponies. The result was the splendid Lipizzaner. These are the original horses of the famous Spanish Riding School in Vienna. In the summer, visitors can watch the horses and their riders give dressage performances (Apr–Oct Tue, Fri and Sun 3pm). Riding lessons are available on request. Adjoining the stud farm is a golf course *(see page 89)*.

Štanjel

The medieval fortified hilltop settlement of **Štanjel** is considered one of the most beautiful villages in Slovenia. It lies 18km (11 miles) northwest of Divača, and within the protective walls, entered through an arched gate, sits a huddle of stone cottages and the 16th-century, Baroque-Renaissance **Štanjel Castle** (Grad Štanjel). It was badly damaged during World War II, but one wing houses the **Lojze Spacal Gallery** (Galerija Lojze Spacala; summer Tue–Fri 10am–2pm, Sat–Sun 10am–6pm, winter Tue–Fri 11am–2pm, Sat–Sun 11am–5pm), displaying an impressive collection of karst-inspired paintings and graphics by Trieste-born Spacal. The entrance ticket is valid for the nearby 15th-century stone **Karst House** (Kraška hiša; open as Gallery), a classic example of local folk architecture.

Hrastovlje

The tiny Romanesque **Church of the Holy Trinity** (Cerkev svete Trojice) at **Hrastovlje**, 31km (19 miles) south of Divača, [14] is nestled in 16th-century defensive walls, built against the Turks. The interior is entirely covered with 15th-century frescos depicting scenes from the Bible, such as the *Creation*, the *Journey of the Magi* and the *Last Judgement*. Painted in 1490 by Janez iz Kastva, they were only rediscovered beneath several layers of whitewash in the 1950s. The best-known piece is the *Danse Macabre* (Dance of Death), showing how, regardless of social status, we are all equal in the face of death. There is also a *Calendar Cycle*, portraying the duties and rituals that took place during each month of the year, leaving a vivid picture of how people once lived in this rural area. The church is usually open, but if it is locked, call at house No.30 in the village and ask for the key. Inside the church, a 20-minute taped commentary is available in several languages.

The Church of the Holy Trinity

THE COAST

The scenic Slovenian coast stretches 47km (26 miles) between Croatia and Italy, where budget airlines bring visitors via Trieste. The tideless waters are clean and clear, and ideal for swim-

Izola, a fishing town on Slovenia's small patch of coast

ming. The local dialect, cuisine and architecture are distinctly Italian, the legacy of Venetian rule. The tourist centres of Portorož (Portorose in Italian) and Piran (Pirano) are packed with hotels, restaurants and marinas, while the industrial port of Koper (Capodistria), 105km (63 miles) southwest of Ljubljana, is often overlooked but has a magnificent historic centre.

Koper

Koper is Slovenia's main port. Tourists often pass it by, considering it too industrial, but the medieval **old town** has Slovenia's most beautiful buildings from the Venetian era. Hard to imagine today, the city was an island that was not joined to the mainland until a landfill in the 19th century. Koper was founded by the ancient Greeks as Aegida, renamed Capris by the Romans, then became Byzantine Justinopolis. In 1279 it was taken by the Venetians, who made it the capital of Venetian Istria, hence its Italian name, 'Capo d'Istria'. By the 16th-century the population had reached 10,000. 15

Koper's most impressive monuments are found in the well-preserved old town on **Tito's Square** (Titov trg). On the north side stands the 17th-century Venetian-Gothic **loggia** (Loža). Its ground-floor Loggia Café is a perfect spot for coffee while enjoying the view across the square. Opposite the loggia, the **Praetorian Palace** (Pretorska palača) is a hotch potch of Venetian-Gothic and Renaissance styles. It was built as the residence of Koper's *podesta* (mayor), and the seat of the Grand Council. A tourist information centre occupies the ground floor. On the square's eastern side is the **Cathedral of the Assumption** (Stolnica Marijinega vnebovzetja; daily 7am–noon and 4–7pm), dating back to the 12th century, and combining Venetian-Gothic and Renaissance elements. Visitors can climb the 36m (118ft) belltower (daily 10am–1pm and 4–7pm) for stunning views over the Gulf of Trieste. Behind the cathedral is the 12th-century circular baptistery.

West of Titov trg, the **Koper Regional Museum** (Pokrajinski muzej Koper, Kidričeva 1; June–Aug Tue–Fri 9am–7pm, Sat–Sun 9am–1pm; Sept–May Tue–Fri 9am–5pm, Sat–Sun 9am– 1pm; charge; www.pmk-kp.si) displays an assortment of stone carvings from local churches, period furniture and paintings, plus a fine copy of the *Danse Macabre* from the Holy Trinity in Hrastovlje *(see page 57)*.

Koper's Praetorian Palace, where the Grand Council sat

East of Titov trg, close to the former town walls, the **Ethnological Collection** (Etnološki zbirka, Gramšijev trg 4; May–Oct Tue–Fri noon–7pm; charge) is housed in a 14th-century Venetian-Gothic building. The exhibition highlights the local use of stone in building and sculpture from the 17th century onwards.

Izola and Strunjan

Izola, 6km (4 miles) south of Koper, is an easy-going fishing town, built on a small peninsula jutting out to sea. As the name suggests, the town was once an island; it was joined to the mainland in the 19th century. The old town is made up of narrow streets lined with Venetian-style, pastel-coloured buildings.

Although appealing, there's little in the way of cultural interest, and most people come here simply to enjoy the sea and sunshine, to sail from the large marina on the edge of town, or to party – Izola has Slovenia's largest and best-known nightclub, **Ambasada Gavioli** *(see page 95)*.

Lying between Izola and Piran, **Strunjan** is a 4km (2½-mile) stretch of coast backed by dramatic cliffs giving onto a pebble beach popular with nudists. Strunjan Bay was once an important salt-making area, and the saltpans can still be made out today. West of Strunjan lie a campsite and the Strunjan Health Resort, offering healing therapies using mud from the former saltpans. The 160ha (395-acre) **Strunjan Nature Reserve** includes a 200m (650ft) wide coastal water belt to protect marine species.

Piran

16 **Piran** is Slovenia's most beautiful coastal town. Sitting compact on a small pointed peninsula, the old town is composed of pastel-coloured Venetian-Gothic buildings presided over by a hilltop church. The town's name is derived from the

Beautiful Venetian-era Piran on Slovenia's coast

Greek *pyr* (fire), after the fire that was lit on the tip of the peninsula to guide galleys into the port at nearby Aegida (Koper) 10km (6 miles) away. In the 5th century AD, Romans fleeing to the coast to escape the Huns settled here. For some 500 years, from 1283 to 1797, Piran came under Venetian rule, which produced splendid buildings and a proud maritime status. The Republic was supplied with salt from the nearby saltpans. Subsequent relative neglect under the Habsburgs preserved the delightful medieval atmosphere.

Today, Piran's main public meeting point is the white marble, oval-shaped **Tartini Square** (Tartinijev trg), which was the inner harbour until 1864 when it was filled in. It is named after the musician Giuseppe Tartini *(see page 62)*, and his bronze statue is at its centre.

He was born in the yellow house (No. 7), where the **Tartini Memorial Room** occupies the first floor (Tartinijeva spominska soba; Tue–Sun July–Aug 9am–noon and 6–9pm,

Sept–May 11am–noon and 5–6pm; charge; www.portoroz. si). It contains his death mask, violin and music manuscripts.

Tartini Square opens onto the fishing harbour, and beyond it is the **Prešernovo nabrežje** promenade, lined with seafood restaurants. On the hill above town is the 17th-century Baroque **Church of St George** (Cerkev svetega Jurija). Its freestanding belltower resembles a smaller version of Venice's San Marco campanile. If you are lucky enough to find it open, climb to the top for stunning views over the Gulf of Trieste.

A few steps west of Tartinjev trg, at Kidričevo nabrežje 4, is the **Aquarium** (July–Aug daily 9am–10pm, Sept–June daily 10am–noon and 2–7pm). Here, a series of well-lit pools exhibit various flora and fauna from the Adriatic Sea.

Overlooking the harbour at Cankarjevo nabrežje 3, the **Sergej Mašera Maritime Museum** (Pomorski muzej Sergej Mašera; July–Aug Tue–Sun 9am–noon, 6–9pm, Sept–June Tue–Sun 9am–5pm; charge) traces Piran's naval history and maritime past.

Giuseppe Tartini

Violinist and composer Giuseppe Tartini (1692–1770) was born in Piran and attended school in nearby Koper. Against the wishes of his parents, who wanted him to become a Franciscan monk, he went to Padua in Italy to study law. At 18 he eloped with Elizabetta Premazone, the Bishop of Padua's niece. After three years the couple were found. To escape persecution Tartini fled to the Convent of St Francis in Assisi where he started playing the violin. Pardoned, he returned to Padua to set up a violin school, attracting students from all over Europe. He composed more than 130 pieces for violin. The best known, a solo sonata called *The Devil's Trill*, was written after he dreamed the devil was playing the violin. He is buried next to his wife in Padua.

Portorož

Violinist Giuseppe Tartini's statue in Tartini Square, Piran

Piran is connected to **Portorož** by a coastal promenade, overlooked by several large modern hotels. People have been coming to the 'port of roses' for health treatments since the 13th century, when Benedictine monks started curing diseases with the sea water and mineral-rich mud from local saltpans. In the late 19th century, Portorož established itself as a health centre and aristocratic tourist resort. Today it is a commercial resort, with a beach of imported sand lined with sunloungers and parasols, and a row of large upmarket hotels offering health and beauty treatments. The most exclusive is the Grand Hotel Portorož *(see page 140)*.

Sečovlje

South of Portorož, close to the Croatian border, on the **Sečovlje Saltpans**, lies the **Saltworks Museum** (Muzej solinarstva; daily Apr–May and Sept–Oct 9am–6pm, June–Aug 9am–8pm; charge). Set in a flat, wet landscape straddled by dykes, these pans were begun in the 13th century and covered 650ha (1,600 acres). They were abandoned in 1967. Each year, local saltworkers left their winter homes to live in stone cottages on the saltpans from spring to early autumn. Three of the original 400 cottages have been restored to form the museum, and tools used for work in the saltpans are displayed here.

NORTHEAST

A world apart from the Mediterranean seascapes and alpine mountains of western Slovenia, the northeast is typically Central European. Here, the influences of Vienna and Budapest are apparent in the architecture, the cuisine and the wines. The main cities are Maribor, Ptuj and Celje, each one with a castle, recording the centuries lived in fear of Turkish attack. The region also offers wine cellars open for tasting, wine roads leading through rural vineyard country, and several modern thermal spas.

Kamnik and Velika Planina

From Ljubljana, the A1 leads northeast to Maribor, then on towards the Hungarian border. En route, a popular detour is **Kamnik**, 23km (14 miles) northeast of the capital. A pretty

Watching the mountain weather, Velika planina

medieval town below the Kamnik Alps (Kamniške Alpe), Kamnik is a popular base for hikers due to the proximity of Velika planina. In the handsome Renaissance-Baroque **Zaprice Castle** (Zaprice grad, really a grand manor house) is the **Kamnik Museum** (Kamniški muzej; Tue–Fri 8am–1pm and 4–7pm, Sat 10am–1pm and 4–6pm, Sun 10am–1pm; charge), presenting the way people in the region lived in the 19th century.

Velika planina (www.velikaplanina.si) is a green mountain plateau 5km (3 miles) north of Kamnik, accessible by cable-car and ski lift. Traditionally the area was given over to dairy farming, but due to its natural beauty this has been superseded by tourism. From spring to autumn visitors can enjoy hiking through the alpine meadows dotted with small settlements of wooden, shingle-roof circular huts. In winter, skiing and night-time sledging are possible.

Volčji Potok Arboretum (4km/2½ miles south of Kamnik; daily 8am–6pm, summer to 8pm; charge; www.arboretum.si) occupies beautifully landscaped grounds, and is home to over 3,500 species and varieties of conifers, deciduous trees and wild herbaceous plants. There is a neat French garden and informal English park, plus an 18-hole golf course.

Logar Valley

The **Logar Valley** (Logarska dolina) is a stunning green glacial valley 34km (21 miles) northeast of Kamnik, with rugged peaks reaching 2,000m (6,560 ft) on each side. The **Logar Valley Trail** is a clearly marked, 7km (4½-mile) path, leading to the 90m (295ft) high **Rinka Waterfall** (Slap Rinka). On the way, it traces the story of the glacial origins of the valley, its wildlife and the way local people have lived over the centuries. The information hut at the entry point can supply visitors with details about organised hiking tours, horse riding, rock climbing and mountain biking. 17

Celje, the third-largest city

Celje

Slovenia's third-largest city was built by the Romans in the 1st century AD as Celeia, a prosperous, densely populated, walled town on the Roman road from Aquileia to Pannonia on the River Savinja 74km (46 miles) northeast of Ljubljana. **Celje** (pronounced *tselyeh*) enjoyed a second period of glory as a principality under the wealthy Counts of Celje during the Middle Ages. In 1456 it came under the Habsburgs, where it remained until 1918.

Today, despite its disconcerting industrial suburbs, it warrants a day's sightseeing. The ruins of the medieval **Old Castle** (Stari grad; free access) perched on a 400m (1,300ft) high rock, 2km (1 mile) southeast of town, is Celje's best-known landmark and the largest castle complex in Slovenia. Built by the Counts of Celje, one of Central Europe's most powerful noble families, the ruins are set within extensive walls. The most intact building is the 14th-century, four-storey **Frederick's Tower** (Friderikov stolp), from which there are excellent views. In summer, medieval re-enactments are staged here.

Celje's other sights lie in the old town, a pleasant provincial mix of Renaissance, Baroque and 20th-century buildings and squares. At Prešernova 17, the **Museum of Modern His-**

tory (Muzej novejše zgodovine; Tue–Fri 10am–6pm, Sat 9am–1pm, Sun 2–6pm; charge; www.muzej-nz-ce.si) examines life in 20th-century Celje. The Children's Museum here has toys, prams, plus a workshop and playroom.

Close to the river in a fine Renaissance building, at Muzejski trg 1, the **Celje Regional Museum** (Pokrajinski muzej Celje; Mar–Oct Tue–Sun 10am–6pm, Nov–Feb Tue–Fri 10am–4pm, Sat 9am–1pm; charge; www.pokmuz-ce.si) is noted for the **Celje Ceiling**, decorated with early 17th-century frescos. Haunting highlights of the rest of the eclectic exhibition are skulls of 18 Counts of Celje.

For evidence of Celje's Roman past, visit **Šempeter**, 12km (8 miles) west of town. Here, along a 300m (1,000ft) long section of the Roman road that once ran between Ljubljana and Celje, is the **Roman Necropolis** (Rimska nekropola; mid-Apr–Sept daily 10am–6pm, Oct Sat–Sun 10am–4pm; charge; www.td-sempeter.si), which has well-preserved, 1st–3rd century AD marble tombs of local Roman dignitaries.

Thirsty travellers might call at **Laško**, 11km (8 miles) south of Celje, renowned throughout Slovenia for making the country's favourite beer, Laško Zlatorog. To request a tour of the brewery contact the Laško Tourist Board; tel: 03-733 89 50, www.turisticnodrustvo-lasko.si. Each year in mid-July Laško celebrates its beer with the five-day Beer and Flowers (Pivo in Cvetje) festival. The town is also known for its thermal springs, and visitors come here to enjoy the indoor and outdoor pools, as well as the saunas.

Rogaška Slatina

Slovenia's oldest and most visited spa town is **Rogaška Slatina**, 36km (23 miles) east of Celje, close to the Croatian border. During the 19th century, the thermal-mineral waters of this elegant retreat attracted an illustrious list of European 18

Mineral miracles

Rogaška Slatina's wealth is built on its mineral water, Donat Mg, on sale throughout Slovenia and exported abroad. Loaded with magnesium, it is said to cure metabolic problems such as obesity, constipation, heartburn and high glucose levels, as well as stress-related diseases and high blood pressure.

aristocrats, including the Habsburgs, the Bourbons and the Bonapartes. Today it offers luxurious health and beauty treatments, as well as being one of the top spas in Central Europe for the treatment of metabolic disorders.

The town centres on Zdraviliški trg, a large square with neatly kept gardens, overlooked by 19th-century neoclassical buildings, plus a few more recent additions. Here you will find the public **Drinking Hall** (daily 7am–1pm and Mon–Sat 3–7pm, Sun 4–7pm; charge), where the highly esteemed local mineral water, Donat Mg, surges directly from a spring.

For a thorough pampering, the place to go is the **Lotus Wellness Centre** (tel: 03-811 40 00; www.rogaska.si), which was opened in 2003 in the Grand Hotel Sava *(see page 142)*. Reservations are necessary for massage, hydrotherapy and beauty treatments. **The Rogaška Riviera complex** (Zdraviliški trg 12, Mon–Fri 9am–8.00pm, Sat 9am–11pm; charge; www.terme-rogaska.si) has pools filled with thermal water, Turkish, Finnish and infrared saunas, a solarium and it also offers massages.

Rogaška Slatina is also known for its crystal glass. Visitors can view and buy glass items from the Rogaška Glassworks' **Tempel** shop at Zdraviliški trg 22, on the main square.

Maribor

Slovenia's second-largest city, **Maribor**, is on the left bank of the River Drava, 126km (79 miles) northeast of Ljubljana. Its origins can be traced to the 12th century, when a fortress (no longer in existence) was erected on Piramida Hill to protect the region against the Magyars. A market grew up outside the castle walls, and town status was granted in 1254. Maribor became an important trade centre, with wine and timber transported on the River Drava by raft. In 1846, when railways linked the city first with Vienna and then with Ljubljana, Maribor won its long-standing rivalry with neighbouring Ptuj *(see page 71)*. While the city is more geared towards business travellers than tourists, the old town – an attractive, well-preserved cluster of coloured Baroque façades and steep terracotta tile roofs – is worth investigation.

Maribor's most prominent sight is the handsome 15th-century **City Castle** (Mestni grad), which houses the **Maribor Regional Museum** (Pokrajinski muzej Maribor; Tue–Sat 9am–4pm, Sun 9am–2pm; charge; www.pmuzej-mb.si). The ornate interior contains a horde of painting and sculpture, regional costumes, objects representing various guilds, wine-making tools, and archaeological finds.

The rooftops of Maribor

Maribor's Plague Pillar

Close by, at Trg svobode 3, lie the **Vinag Wine Cellars** (open to the public for wine tasting, reservations necessary; tel: 02-220 81 11, www.vinag.si). These impressive cellars are among the largest in Central Europe. Around 2.5km (1½ miles) of tunnels store 5.5 million litres (1.2 million gallons) of wine, mainly whites, including the esteemed Plenina Royal, a sparkling wine made by the traditional champagne process.

On the southern edge of the old town, close to the river, lies the **Main Square** (Glavni trg), where the ornate **Plague Pillar** (Kužno znamenje) commemorates a plague that killed a third of the population in 1680–81. The square's most prominent building is the grey-and-white 16th-century **Town Hall** (Rotovž). West of the Main Square, the colourful **Vodnik Square** (Vodnikov trg) holds the open-air market (Mon–Sat 7am–2pm).

Along the southern edge of the old town is the **River Drava**, a tributary of the Danube. Here, Lent is a waterside promenade beside the former port area, where boats sailing from Austria to the Black Sea were once obliged to stop for one night and pay port tax. Today, stages are set up in summer along the riverfront for the spectacular Lent Festival *(see page 97)*. Giving onto the river, at Vojašniška 8, **Stara trta** is a 400-year-old grapevine that has placed Maribor in the *Guinness Book of Records*, as the world's oldest continually producing vine.

Out of town, **Maribor Island** (Mariborski otok) makes a popular summer bathing spot. Lying 5km (3 miles) west of the old town, it can be reached on foot or by bicycle along the riverside promenade. The island is accessed by a bridge and has two outdoor pools (June–Sept 9am–8pm; charge).

The hills of **Maribor Pohorje** (www.pohorje.org), 7km (4 miles) southwest of Maribor and accessible by cable-car, support one of Slovenia's largest winter ski resorts, as well as offering hiking and mountain-biking possibilities. Here, the **Bike Park Pohorje** (daily 10am–6pm, until 7pm summer Thur–Sun; charge; www.bikeparkpohorje.si) challenges cycling enthusiasts with a 4km (2½-mile) downhill run.

Ptuj

The flat fertile flood plain of the River Drava separates Maribor from **Ptuj** 25km (15 miles) away. Commanding a hilltop 19

The cobbled streets of Ptuj, a town known for its carnival

position above the plain, Ptuj was founded by the Romans in the 1st century AD as Poetovio and had 40,000 inhabitants. In 450 it was plundered by the Huns and in the 6th century the site was occupied by the Avars. It passed into the Frankish Empire in the late 8th century, then coming under the Archbishopric of Salzburg, before falling under the Habsburgs in 1555. When neighbouring Maribor was linked by railway to Vienna in the late 19th century, Ptuj fell into relative decline. Today, the old town, filled with cobbled streets lined with Gothic and Baroque buildings and crowned by a hilltop castle, is known throughout Slovenia for its *Kurentovanje* carnival celebrations.

To learn more about Ptuj's ancient past, visit the former **Dominican Monastery** (Dominikanski samostan; mid-Apr–Nov 9am–5pm; charge; www.pok-muzej-ptuj.si) on Muzejski trg, where a small archaeological collection includes fragments from three Roman shrines to Mithras, and collections of coins and gems.

Roman relics aside, Ptuj's most impressive sight has to be **Ptuj Castle** (Grad Ptuj), standing on a hill above town and centring on an elegant Baroque courtyard. The castle

Kurentovanje

Carnival celebrations in Ptuj, known as *Kurentovanje*, take place in the 10 days running up to Shrove Tuesday. This raucous street party involves local men dressing up as Kurent (or Korant), a god of hedonism. These *kurenti* are clad in sheepskin cloaks with cowbells hung around their waists, and wear terrifying masks with beaky noses, large white teeth and protruding bright-red tongues. The men rampage through the streets, from house to house, making a terrible din with their bells. The tradition apparently harks back to pagan fertility rites: the *kurenti* are supposed to chase out the winter and welcome in the spring.

dates from the 12th century, though its present appearance is the result of alterations carried out between the 15th and 18th centuries. Today it houses the highly enjoyable **Ptuj Regional Museum** (Pokrajinski muzej Ptuj; mid-Oct–Apr 9am–5pm, daily May–mid-Oct 9am–6pm, Sat and Sun Jul–Aug until 8pm; charge; www.pok-muzej-ptuj.si), displaying a fine collection of musical instruments, period furniture and traditional *Kurentovanje* (carnival) costumes.

An old wine press

Those who enjoy a drop of fine wine should also arrange a visit to the **Vinska klet** (Wine Cellars; Trstenjakova 6; tel: 02-787 98 10; book at least a day in advance). The standard tour includes a look round the vast cellars, a film about wine-making in the region, and a wine-tasting session.

Wine Roads around Ptuj

The grape-growing Haloze Hills lie south of Ptuj, close to the border with Croatia. The **Haloze Hills Wine Road** begins at **Borl Castle**, overlooking the River Drava 11km (7 miles) southeast of Ptuj. The region produces some of Slovenia's best white wines, and along the route there are several vineyards and wine cellars open to the public.

First stop in the Haloze Hills is the village of **Ptujska Gora**, 12km (8 miles) southwest of Ptuj beneath the 15th-century **Church of the Virgin Mary** (Cerkev svete Marije), a popular pilgrimage site attracting 60,000 visitors annually and offering fine views over the River Drava flood plain.

The **Jeruzalem–Ljutomer Wine Road** lies in the undulating hills northeast of Ptuj, running 18km (11 miles) from Ljutomer to **Ormož**, passing through the hilltop village of **Jeruzalem**, named by the Knights of the Cross who lived here in the 12th century.

Murska Sobota

Pomurje means 'across the Mura', and it is indeed on the far side of the River Mura, close to the Hungarian border. The region is characterised by flat, fertile fields and small farming villages, and there is a sizeable Hungarian minority.

Pomurje's chief urban centre is **Murska Sobota**, on the River Ledava. For insight into local life, visit the **Regional Museum** (Pokrajinski muzej; Tue–Fri 9am–5pm, Sat–Sun 9am–1pm; charge; www.pok-muzej-ms.si) in an 18th-century mansion in the City Park (Mestni Park), where there is an award-winning exhibition.

Moravske Toplice

Another of Slovenia's sophisticated spas, **Moravske Toplice** lies 8km (5 miles) northeast of Murska Sobota. Here, the vast, modern Terme 3000 Spa (daily 8am–9pm; charge; www.terme3000.si) is an aquatic recreation centre, comprising 11 indoor and outdoor pools with geysers, waterfalls, water massage, upstream swimming and bubble-baths. There is a diving pool with a hair-raising 22m (72ft) high platform, plus Turkish and Finnish saunas. A recent addition to the complex is the **Thermalium** (daily 8am–5pm; charge), with 'black' thermal water, said to relax and replenish body and soul, improve circulation and reduce nervous agitation.

On the edge of the resort lie the greens of the 18-hole Livada Golf Course *(see page 90)*. The flat, rural terrain makes the area ideal for cycling. The Bike Centre (www.pomurjeonbike.com) at Kranjčeva 12 hires bicycles and can arrange rafting trips on the River Mura.

SOUTHEAST

Many visitors pass through the southeast region en route from Ljubljana to Zagreb in Croatia without stopping. However, this is to overlook a number of small spa towns, watersports on the River Krka, and several impressive monasteries, castles and wine cellars open to the public.

Stična Monastery

Stična Monastery (Samostan Stična; daily monastery 8am–noon and 2–5pm – you will be guided around – and museum 8am–5pm; tel: 01-787 78 63; www.mks-sticna.si) is set amid green meadows close to Ivančna Gorica, 32km (22 miles) from Ljubljana on the A2. Founded by the Cistercians in 1135, Stična is the oldest monastery in Slovenia. In the 15th century it was fortified with high walls against 20

Stična Monastery

Turkish attack, and became the region's main religious, economic, educational and cultural centre. In 1784 it was closed by the Habsburgs, who believed the monasteries had become too powerful, but it reopened in 1898. Today a dozen monks are in residence.

Tours begin with a 20-minute audio-visual presentation, then pass through the **Slovenian Museum of Christianity** (Muzej krščanstva na Slovenskem), displaying religious paintings, icons, manuscripts, processional crosses and chalices, as well as objects related to the monks' work, such as bookbinding and farming. Visitors are also shown the Baroque **monastery church** and the 13th-century Gothic vaulted cloisters, and the tour ends with a look in the monastery shop selling herbal teas, tinctures and ointments prepared to recipes devised by the late Father Simon Ašič, plus wine and honey made by the monks, and religious souvenirs.

Novo Mesto

Southeast Slovenia's largest town and cultural centre of the Dolenjska region is **Novo mesto** (www.novomesto.si), 55km (34 miles) east of Ljubljana on the A2. In medieval times it was a market town and trading centre, and today it is an important industrial zone and home to the pharmaceutical company Krka. The old town lies compact in a meander on the left bank of the River Krka, accessed by three bridges.

Novo mesto on the River Krka

Dolenjska Museum (Dolenjski muzej; Tue–Sat 9am–5pm, Sun 9am–1pm; charge; www.dolmuzej.com) at Mu-

A Dolenjska Museum exhibit about Partisans in World War II

zejska 7, has a highly regarded archaeological collection with Iron and Bronze Age finds, notably *situlae* – ornately decorated bronze urns found in burial sites nearby. There are cultural history, recent history and ethnological collections, and a permanent collection of art from the 17th to 20th centuries, of which the most prized item is a miniature three-sectioned portable altar from 1652.

Café life centres on the main square, **Glavni trg**, a long cobbled piazza, more a street than a square, surrounded by 16th-century vaulted arcades, which originally housed craft workshops and merchants' stores.

Just off the south end of Glavni trg, near the river, the **Božidar Jakac House** (Jakčev dom; Tue–Sat 9am–5pm, last Sun of the month 9am–1pm; charge; www.dolmuzej.com) displays sketches and paintings by distinguished local artist Božidar Jakac (1899–1989). The ground and first floors are devoted to pictures of the region's landscape and inhabitants, while the second floor exhibits paintings from the artist's journeys in Europe and America.

Also worth a look is the **Chapter Church of St Nicholas** (Cerkev svetega Nikolaja), which dates from the 14th century and is Novo mesto's oldest surviving building. A highlight is a fine painting of St Nicholas by the renowned Venetian artist Tintoretto (1518–94).

Dolenjske Toplice

The small Austro-Hungarian-style spa town of **Dolenjske Toplice**, 12km (8 miles) southwest of Novo mesto, has recently acquired the large, modern **Balnea Wellness Centre**, with indoor and outdoor pools (Sun–Thur 9am–9pm, Fri–Sat 9am–11pm; charge; www.terme-krka.si), waterfalls and geysers, a sophisticated range of relaxing saunas (from 11am), plus beauty treatments and massage (daily 9am–9pm). For those who prefer adventure sports, there is the possibility of rafting, kayaking or canoeing on the River Krka *(see page 88)*.

Otočec

The impressive Gothic-Renaissance **Otočec Castle** (Grad Otočec), 7km (4 miles) east of Novo mesto, has been refurbished to make the Otočec Castle Hotel *(see page 142)*. Built with four towers, it lies on an island on the River Krka, and is accessed by a wooden bridge. Although it is not open to the public, non-residents are welcome in the upmarket restaurant and café. Otočec Golf Course *(see page 90)* and the Struga Equestrian Centre both lie close to the castle.

In early July each year, the castle grounds hold Rock Otočec (www.rock-otocec.com), a three-day rock festival that attracts some 8,000 visitors daily. Past performers include Fun Lovin' Criminals and Asian Dub Foundation, though in recent years more emphasis has been given to any bands coming from the countries of former Yugoslavia.

Pleterje Monastery

In a peaceful valley close to the small village of Šentjernej, some 20km (12½ miles) east of Otočec, lies

21 **Pleterje Monastery** (Samostan Pleterje; www.kartuzija-pleterje.si). Hidden amid dense woodland and vineyards, the monastery was founded in the 15th century. It was fortified against the Turks, only to be lost by the Carthusians in 1593. It was repurchased and reopened in 1904, and is home to about a dozen Carthusian monks. As the Carthusians value silence and solitude, most of Pleterje is closed to visitors. However, it is possible to view the magnificent 15th-century Gothic **Church of the Holy Trinity** (Cerkev svete Trojice; daily 9am–5.30pm; charge) and watch a short film about the way the monks live – they practise collective labour, solitary contemplation and abstain from meat. The monastery also owns a fine collection of old master paintings, but these are now displayed in the Božidar Jakac Gallery in Kostanjevica na Krki *(see page 81)*.

Otočec Castle

A shop (closed Sunday) next to the church sells goods produced by the monks, such as wine, potent local spirits – including *viljamovka*, with a whole pear inside the bottle, and *slivovka* made from plums – as well as honey, propolis, mead (honey wine) and beeswax candles. Visitors can also walk the 4km (2½-mile) **Pleterje Way**, following a marked path – look out for a blue circle and a yellow cross – around the perimeter of the complex, which the monks do on their weekly outing when they are allowed to break their vow of silence.

In the woods, close to the entrance to the monastery, lies the **Pleterje Open-Air Museum** (Muzej na prostem Pleterje; Mar–Oct daily 9am–5pm; charge; www.skansen.si). This reconstruction of a 19th-century traditional farm includes a wooden, thatch-roof farmhouse with period furniture, several wooden outbuildings, a potter's workshop, and a stone well. There is a small souvenir shop, and the complex puts on occasional demonstrations of local crafts.

Pleterje Monastery

Kostanjevica na Krki

On an island in a deep curve in the River Krka, accessed via two bridges, is the tiny town of **Kostanjevica na Krki**. Some 6km (4 miles) east of Šentjernej, it dates from the 11th century and has been designated a cultural monument. With just two main streets and a couple of small Gothic churches, it makes an unusual and photogenic destination.

On the southwest of the village at Grajska 45, a disused 13th-century Cistercian

Self portrait by local artist Božidar Jakac (1899–1989)

monastery now houses the **Božidar Jakac Gallery** (Galerija Božidar Jakac; Apr–Oct Tue–Sun 9am–6pm, Nov–Mar Tue–Sun 9am–4pm; charge; www.galerija-bj.si). The collection displays paintings by 20th-century Slovenian artists, including several fine pastels and oils by Božidar Jakac, who founded the gallery in 1974 and was one of the initiators of the Ljubljana Academy of Fine Arts. There is also a permanent exhibition of 44 paintings by French, Flemish, Italian and German Old Masters belonging to Pleterje Monastery. In the grounds, wooden sculptures from the international open-air sculpture symposium Forma Viva are on display.

Brežice

The picturesque little town of **Brežice** lies 15km (10 miles) east of Kostanjevica na Krki at the point where the River Krka flows into the River Sava. It is well worth a stop to visit the 16th-century Renaissance **Brežice Castle** housing the excellent **Brežice Posavski Museum** (Posavski muzej Brežice; Mon–Fri 8am–2.30pm, Sat–Sun 10am–2pm; charge; www.posavski-muzej.si), some parts are under extensive renovation. The highlight is the Knights' Hall, decorated with exceptional Baroque frescos that create optical illusions. But the museum itself is also interesting, tracing the region's history from the earliest Roman and Celtic settlers to World War II.

Each summer the Knights' Hall and the castle courtyard host the Brežice Festival of Early Music (mid-June to mid-Aug; www.seviqc-brezice.si), with ancient and Baroque music.

The **Brežice Bicycle Trail**, which begins and ends in Brežice, is a 97km (61-mile) long round trip with 10 checkpoints of either natural or cultural interest, including the spa town of Čatež and the wine-making village of Bizeljsko, 19km (12 miles) northeast of the town.

Bizeljsko

Close to the Croatian border, **Bizeljsko** is known for its unusual *repnice* wine cellars. These underground chambers were originally dug for storing turnips (*repa* means turnip in Slovenian), but their constant low temperatures and humidity also make them perfect for maturing wine, which is what they are mainly used for today. **Vino Graben** (Kumrovška 6; tel: 07-495 1059; Fri–Sun 9am–7pm, other days by agreement; www.vino-graben.com) offers tastings and the chance to visit some *repnice* cellars. The Vino Graben order book includes such elite customers as former US president Bill Clinton and several European royal families.

Čatež

Slovenia's largest natural health resort, **Čatež** (www.terme-catez.si) is 24km (15 miles) east of Novo mesto on the A2, and just 3km (2 miles) southeast of Brežice. Built over underground thermal springs, Čatež was founded in the 1920s, but only really developed into a serious spa resort in the 1960s. Today it has a selection of modern hotels and receives some 640,000 visitors annually, some of whom come for health treatments and to relax and recharge.

The **Thermal Riviera** is a vast, ultra-modern complex consisting of the **Summer Thermal Riviera**, a huge open-air water park (daily 9am–7pm; charge) comprising seven

Čatež, Slovenia's largest health resort

thermal pools (average temperature 30°C/86°F) with wave machines, waterfalls and slides; plus the indoor **Winter Thermal Riviera** (daily 9am–9pm; charge), with yet more pools hosting slides, wave machines, water massage machines and whirlpools. Another attraction is the large **Sauna Park** (Mon–Fri 11am–9pm, Sat–Sun 10am–9pm; charge), offering an extravagant selection of eight kinds of sauna.

Mokrice Castle

The Renaissance **Mokrice Castle**, 8km (5 miles) southeast of Čatež, has been refurbished to accommodate the classy Mokrice Castle Golf Hotel *(see page 142)*. Set amid parkland, it is approached over a moat with a drawbridge, and the interior is furnished with period antiques. Although it is not open to the public, non-residents are welcome in the upmarket restaurant. There is also an 18-hole golf course *(see page 90)*, and the hotel offers special packages for golfers.

WHAT TO DO

SPORTS AND OUTDOOR PURSUITS

Soaring mountains, broad lakes and crashing rivers make Slovenia a great place to explore nature and enjoy the outdoor life. The following companies can organise outdoor activities: **3glav Adventures**, Ljubljanska 1, Bled, tel: 04-168 31 84, www.3glav-adventures.com (hiking, cycling, rafting, kayaking and canoeing trips); and **Alpinsport**, Ribčev Laz 53, Bohinj, tel: 04-572 34 86, www.alpinsport.si (hiking, cycling, rafting, kayaking and canoeing trips).

River sports, like rafting, canyoning and hydrospeed, are organised by: **Agency K2M**, Pionirska 3, Doljenske Toplice, tel: 07-306 68 30, www.k2m.si; **Alpe Sport Vančar**, Trg golobarskih žrtev 20, Bovec, tel: 05-389 63 50, www.bovecsport.com; **Bovec Rafting Team**, Bovec, tel: 05-388 61 28, www.bovec-rafting-team.com; **Soča Rafting**, Trg golobarskih žrtev 48, Bovec, tel: 05-389 62 00, www.socarafting.si; **X Point**, Stresova 1, Kobarid, tel: 05-388 53 08, www.xpoint.si.

Skiing

Skiing is the Slovenes' favourite sport. There are both downhill pistes and cross-country trails, and snow from early December to late March. The country has three major annual skiing World Cup competitions: men's alpine skiing in Kranjska Gora; women's alpine events in Maribor; and ski jumping at Planica near Kranjska Gora. **Elan** (www.elansnowboards.com, www.elanskis.com) manufactures world-renowned skis and snowboards. Visit www.slovenia.info and download the 'Slovenia Skiing' brochure.

The mountain scenery is glorious for skiing

The following are the top ski resorts:

Kranjska Gora (www.kranjska-gora.si), the largest and most popular ski resort, lies on the edge of Triglav National Park in the northwest. Excellent for beginners and early intermediates, it is popular with families.

Pohorje (www.pohorje.org), the second-largest resort, lies just outside Maribor. Its 5km (3-mile) night-time lit ski slope is the longest in Europe.

Rogla (www.rogla.si) is a resort with skiing at all levels, but plenty for beginners so is also good for families.

Just outside **Bovec** (www.boveckanin.si), the Kanin Ski Centre is the highest ski resort (altitude 2,300m/7,550ft), and consequently has the longest season.

Vogel (www.vogel.si), above Lake Bohinj, reached via cable-car from Ukanc, has stunning scenery.

Krvavec (www.rtc-krvavec.si), near Kranj and Ljubljana, is popular with day-trippers from the capital. There is little accommodation in the ski area so most stay in the valley.

Hiking

Hiking comes a close second to skiing as the Slovenes' top activity. There are over 7,000km (4,500 miles) of hiking paths, marked at intervals with a white circle in a red circle, usually painted on rocks. There are also 165 mountain huts, managed by the Alpine Association of Slovenia (www.pzs.si), offering basic overnight accommodation. Several UK-based travel agencies offer all-inclusive hiking holidays in Triglav National Park, such as **Naturetrek**,

Scaling Triglav

The top area for hiking is Triglav National Park. Its centrepiece is Mount Triglav (2,864m/9,396ft), the country's highest peak. The most popular base for hikers is Bohinj, not least because it offers the best starting point for climbing Mount Triglav, via Ukanc.

Cyclists at Triglav National Park

tel: 01962 733 051, www.naturetrek.co.uk, and **Ramblers Holidays**, tel: 01707 331 133, www.ramblersholidays.co.uk.

Cycling

Slovenia is considered one of Europe's top mountain-biking destinations, and many visitors come here specifically to cycle through Triglav National Park and the Soča Valley. The Slovenian Tourist Board's pamphlet *Biking in Slovenia* is free from the head office or through the website. Several UK-based travel agencies offer all-inclusive cycling holidays in Slovenia, including **Skedaddle**, tel: 0191 265 1110, www.skedaddle.co.uk, and **2 Wheel Treks**, tel: 0845 612 6106, www.2wheeltreks.co.uk.

Rafting, Kayaking, Canoeing and Canyoning

A series of falls and rapids on the **River Soča** makes it one of the most beautiful and challenging rivers in Europe for rafting, kayaking, canoeing and hydrospeed. The main bases are Bovec and Kobarid. In addition, the **River Krka**, in the southeast, makes a fine venue for watersports, albeit on slightly tamer waters. The Soča Valley is also the top venue for canyoning, and the main base is at Bovec. Routes range from beginners to extreme canyoning, which includes abseiling. (For agencies that organise river sports, *see page 85*).

Fishing

The top places for fishing are the **River Soča** (where Kobarid makes a perfect base), **Lake Bohinj** in Triglav National Park, and the **River Krka** in the southeast. The **Fisheries Research Institute of Slovenia** (Zavod za Ribištvo Slovenije; Župančičeva 9, Ljubljana; tel: 01-244 34 05; www.zzrs.si) provides information about seasons and permits.

Extreme Sports Achievements

In contrast to the other countries of former Yugoslavia, which have achieved international success in team sports such as football and basketball, Slovenes have always excelled in individual sports. In 2000, Davo Karničar became the first man to ski the whole way down Mount Everest, from an altitude of 8,850m (29,035ft) down to the base camp at 5,340m (17,500ft) in just under five hours. In the same year, professional marathon swimmer Martin Strel swam the entire 3,004km (1,867-mile) length of the River Danube in 58 days. In 2001, again on the Danube, he set a new world record for non-stop swimming, covering 500km (313 miles) in 84 hours and 10 minutes. Then, in 2002, he swam 3,797km (2,360 miles) of the Mississippi in North America. Also in 2002, Marko Bahol set a new world record by cycling continuously for 12 hours, clocking up 452km (281 miles) at the Novo mesto Velodrome. All three have earned Slovenia places in the *Guinness Book of Records*.

Sailing

Rafting on the Soča

Slovenia is a perfect launching place for sailing down the Adriatic. The country has three well-equipped marinas: Portorož, Koper and Izola, each of which has been awarded a European Blue Flag for safety, cleanliness and respect for the environment. There are several charter companies offering boats for hire, and if you do not have a sailing licence they will also provide a skipper. They include **Portorož Marina**, Cesta solinarjev 8, tel: 05-676 12 00, www.marinap.si; **Izola Marina**, Tomažičeva 10, tel: 05-662 54 00, www.marinaizola.com; and **Koper Marina**, Kopališko nabrežje 5, tel: 05-662 61 00, www.marina-koper.si. There are also two companies which design and produce world-class yachts: **Elan** (www.elan-yachts.com) and **Seaway** (www.seaway.si).

Golf

The Tourist Board's pamphlet *Golf Courses in Slovenia* is available free from the head office or through the website. There are nine courses. The oldest and the most beautiful is **Golf & Country Club Bled**, www.golfbled.com, near Lake Bled: the nine-hole Lake Course was laid out in 1938, and the splendid 18-hole King's Course was designed by Donald Harradine in 1972. Reservations are needed at least three days in advance. **Lipica**, www.lipica.si, was upgraded from nine-hole to 18-hole in 2007; **Golf Course Arboretum**, www.golf

Enjoying a round of golf

arboretum.si, is an 18-hole course adjoining Volčji Potok Arboretum, near Kamnik; **Golf Grad Mokrice**, www.terme-catez.si, is an 18-hole course laid out in parkland and woods close to Mokrice Castle in the Krka Valley; **Ptuj**, www.golf-ptuj.si, is an 18-hole course noted for its water hazards including two lakes; **Livada**, www.terme3000.si, is a new 18-hole course on the edge of Moravske Toplice spa complex, in the northeast; **Otočec Golf Course**, www.terme-krka.si, is a nine-hole course stretching over hilly terrain along the banks of the River Krka near Otočec Castle; **Zlati Grič**, www.zlati-gric.si, is a nine-hole course among picturesque vineyards in Slovenske Konjice, between Celje and Maribor; **Podčetrtek**, www.terme-olimia.com, near Terme Olimia spa, 35km (22 miles) east of Celje, near Croatia's border, is a nine-hole course.

Horse Riding

The beautiful unspoilt countryside is ideal for trekking. There are several highly professional equestrian schools, the best-known being the **Lipica Stud Farm** *(see page 55)*, tel: 05-739 15 80, www.lipica.org. It offers individual lessons, plus hacking in guided groups. **Ranč. Mrcina**, tel: 04-179 02 97 (mobile), www.ranc-mrcina.com, in Studor, near Lake Bohinj, has Icelandic ponies and Lipizzaner horses for trekking. **Pristava Lepena**, tel: 05-388 99 00, www.pristava-lepena.com, in the Lepena Valley in Triglav National Park, keeps a stable of Lipizzaner horses and gives lessons at all levels, plus group trekking.

Horse riding is also possible at some agrotourism centres.

Spas

Under Austro-Hungarian rule, spa towns became fashionable with the aristocracy. There are 15 spas today, all of which come under the umbrella of the Slovenian Spas Community (www.spa-slovenia.com) and are recognised by the Slovenian National health system.

However, they now offer much more than just medical cures and convalescence, and many have sophisticated wellness centres and water recreation parks. The Slovenian Tourist Board publishes two pamphlets, *Wellness – Tailor-made for You* and *Health Resorts*, both available free from the head office or through the website.

Beaches and Bathing

With just 47km (26 miles) of coast, Slovenian beaches get very crowded in the summer, and many Slovenes prefer to go down to neighbouring Croatia. Visitors should beware of coastal hotels that claim to have a beach: in many cases this is no more than a concrete platform affording easy access into the water. The most organised beach is in Portorož, where a strip of imported sand is lined with sun-loungers and umbrellas. The best natural beaches lie between Piran and Fiesa, and at Strunjan, just north of Fiesa. Strunjan has an area reserved for nudists. The water temperature is ideal for swimming from June to mid-October, though hardy types might manage both earlier and later.

SHOPPING

European high-street names are moving in fast, not least because of the country's sound economy. However, for many foreign visitors the most enjoyable shopping experience remains a visit to the open-air markets, where besides fresh fruit and vegetables, one can purchase locally produced honey, and dried herbs for cooking and preparing tea. The largest and most colourful markets are found in Ljubljana and Maribor.

In Ljubljana you can find upmarket boutiques and antique shops on Mestni trg and Stari trg in the old town, while high-street clothing stores can be found on pedestrian Čopova near the Triple Bridge. In Maribor the main shopping street is Gosposka in the old town, and in Koper Čevljarska, also in the old town. BTC City, a large mall, lies 3km (1½ miles) northeast of Ljubljana city centre and has more than 400 shops, a microbrewery, a multiplex cinema, a sports hall and the Atlantis Waterpark.

Open-air markets

Gifts you might wish to bring back from Slovenia include the **herbal teas** and **honey** made by monks from Stična Monastery, *viljamovka* and *slivovka* (both **fruit-based spirits**) from Pleterje Monastery, **handmade lace**

from Idrija and **crystal glass** from Rogaška Slatina. For quality outdoor sports equipment, try Elan **skis** and **snowboards**, and Planika **hiking boots**.

Craft souvenirs

Local **wines** can be purchased directly from vineyards and wine cellars. The Tourist Board has devised a series of country-wide *vinske ceste* (wine roads), leading directly to cellars open to the public. Wine-tasting sessions normally include a range of the producer's wines, starting with dry *(suho)* varieties and progressing to the sweet *(sladko)* ones, accompanied by salty nibbles such as *pršut* (air-dried ham), cheese and homemade bread. It is often possible to have bottles packed in presentation boxes that make fine gifts. It is advisable to telephone the cellars at least one day in advance to confirm the time of your visit. The following cellars in locations mentioned in this guide are open to the public:

Northeast: Vinska klet, Trstenjakova 6, Ptuj, tel: 02-787 98 10 (book in advance); **Vinag Wine Cellars**, Trg svobode 3, Maribor, tel: 02-220 81 11, www.vinag.si; **Hlebec**, Kog 181, Kog (on the Jeruzalem Wine Road), tel: 02-713 70 60, www.hlebec-kog.net.

Northwest: Vinoteka Brda, Dobrovo Castle, Grajska 10, Dobrovo (16km/10 miles northwest of Nova Gorica), tel: 05-395 92 10, www.vinotekabrda.si; **Goriška Brda wine cellars**, Zadružna cesta 9, Dobrovo, tel: 05-331 01 00, www.klet-brda.com.

Southeast: Vino Graben, Kumrovška 6, Bizeljsko, tel: 07-495 10 59, www.vino-graben.com.

ENTERTAINMENT

Nightlife and Café Culture

A large student population guarantees an animated nightlife in Ljubljana. The most popular bars and cafés lie in the centre, with outdoor tables lining the riverside promenade of Cankarjevo nabrežje, plus an increasing number of lounge and cocktail bars on Mestni trg and Stari trg in the old town. The most popular include **Maček** (Krojaska 5), a long-standing, see-and-be-seen café-bar overlooking the river close to the Triple Bridge; **Café Galerija** (Mestni trg 5), a trendy cocktail bar with a Turkish-style, candlelit interior; **Fraga** (Mestni trg 15), an arty bar with a minimalist interior decorated with modern art; **Movia** (Mestni trg 2), a small, sophisticated, candlelit wine bar with an excellent wine list; and **Makalonca** (Hribarjevo nabrežje 19), a fun bar with DJs playing house, funk and soul indoors, plus outdoor, candlelit tables overlooking the river in summer.

Students enliven Ljubljana

The best dance clubs in the capital are: **Top** (Tomšičeva 2, www.klubtop.si), on the top floor of the *Nama* building with great music, a lively crowd, plus brilliant views of the city; and **Bachus** (Kongresni trg 3, www.bachus-center.com), combining a restaurant, lounge bar, wine bar and dance club on three separate floors. Jazz enthusiasts should check out **Gajo Jazz Bar** (Beethovnova 8, www.jazzclubgajo.com), where local and international musicians perform, while rock fans should head for **Orto** (Grablovičeva 1, www.orto-bar.com) for live concerts. The young, alternative crowd meet at the student-run **Klub K4** (Kersnikova 4, www.klubk4.org) and **Metelkova** (Metelkova, www.metelkova.org), a squat-cum-arts centre.

Coastal clubbing

In summer, late-night revellers head for the coast, where Ambasada Gaviol (www.ambasada-gavioli.net) in Izola is Slovenia's largest club. The country's best-known DJ, Umek, is joined here by an impressive list of international guests.

In **Maribor**, Patrick's J&B Pub (Poštna 10, between Glavni trg and Slomski trg) is a cosy Irish pub which stays open until 2am on Fri and Sat; Jazz Klub Satchmo (Strossmayerjeva 6, www.jazz-klub.si) is an excellent live jazz bar; and Trust (Gosposvetska cesta 84, www.trust.si) is a café-restaurant by day and a lively dance club by night.

During the summer, late-night revellers head for the coast, particularly **Izola** *(see above)*. If a quiet drink is more your thing, try Café Teater (Stjenkova 1) overlooking the harbour in **Piran**, or Loggia Café (Titov trg 1) inside the 17th-century Venetian loggia on the main square in Koper.

Cultural Performances

In **Ljubljana**, Slovenska Filharmonija (Philharmonic Hall), (Kongresni trg 10, tel: 01-241 08 00, www.filharmonija.si) is the top venue for classical music concerts; SNG Opera in Balet Ljubljana (Župančičeva 1, tel: 01-241 17 00, www.opera.si) put on opera and ballet; Cankarjev dom (Trg republike, tel: 01-241 71 00, www.cd-cc.si) is a multi-purpose cultural centre staging concerts, theatre, dance, film and art exhibitions; Kinoteka (Miklošičeva 28, tel: 01-547 15 80, www.kinoteka.si) is an arts cinema; and Klub K4 (Kersnikova 4, www.klubk4.org) is a student-run nightclub with occasional live concerts and theatrical performances.

Beyond the capital, in **Maribor**, the Slovensko narodno gledališče (SNG, Slovenian National Theatre, Slovenska ulica 27, tel: 02-250 61 00, www.sng-mb.si) has theatre and opera, while in **Koper**, Gledališče Koper (Koper Theatre; Verdijeva 3, tel: 05-663 43 80, www.gledalisce-koper.si) is the top venue for drama on the coast.

Throughout summer many towns have cultural festivals. The main ones are the Ljubljana Summer Festival (www.ljubljanafestival.si) in the capital and the Lent Festival (www.maribor-pohorje.si) in Maribor.

CHILDREN'S ACTIVITIES

Mountain walks and picnics, rowing boats on the lakes, and fun on the beaches and in the castles and caves should all keep children happy. Attractions that should particularly appeal include a visit to the beautiful white Lipizzaner horses at the **Lipica Stud Farm**, a tour of the **Idrija Mercury Mine**, and a ride aboard a miniature train through the chambers and tunnels of **Postojna Cave**, filled with stalagmites and stalactites. Remember also that many spas have special areas for children, and some have waterparks with wave machines, waterfalls and slides.

An active holiday

Calendar of Events

January Pohorje ski resort near Maribor holds the World Cup in women's alpine skiing.

February *Kurentovanje* (carnival) celebrations in Ptuj take place during the 10 days running up to Shrove Tuesday.

March Ski Jumping World Championship at Planica near Kranjska Gora.

Late May Druga Godba, alternative-world music festival in Ljubljana.

May to June Exodos festival of contemporary performing arts, Ljubljana.

June Lent Festival, two-week event featuring music, dance and theatre on the banks of the River Drava in Maribor.

June (last weekend) Venus Journey, medieval street festival, Škofja Loka.

June to mid-September Ljubljana Summer Festival: open-air music, dance and theatre.

Mid-June to mid-August Brežice Festival of Early Music. European musicians play ancient and Baroque pieces at Brežice Castle.

Mid-June Bled International Regatta, world-class rowing on Lake Bled.

Late June Idrija hosts a 10-day Lacemaking Festival (Čipkarski festival) with displays and events around town.

Late June to early July Bled International Violin Festival, two-week event.

Early July Ljubljana Jazz Festival, three days of world-class jazz.

Early July Rock Otočec, Slovenia's largest open-air rock festival, runs for three days in the grounds of Otočec Castle near Novo mesto. Past performers include the Asian Dub Foundation and Henry Rollins.

Mid-July Laško celebrates its beer with the five-day Pivo Cvetje (Beer and Flowers) festival.

August Knights' Tournament at Predjama Castle celebrates medieval chivalry.

Mid-August to mid-September Tartini Festival, Piran celebrates the works of the 18th-century violinist and composer, Giuseppe Tartini.

Early September Stara Trta, Ceremonial Grape Harvest, Maribor.

Late October Ljubljana Marathon.

11 November Martinovanje (St Martin's Day) celebrates the year's new wine, with festivities all over the country, most notably in Maribor.

EATING OUT

Slovenian cuisine, like its history, is a delightful blend of Austro-Hungarian and Venetian influences. Expect goodies such as *Dunajski zrezek* (Wiener schnitzel), *golaž* (goulash), *pršut* (prosciutto) and *rižota* (risotto), as well as an array of wholesome Slovenian country dishes guaranteed to fill you up, including *klobasa* (sausage) served with *kislo zelje* (sauerkraut), *krvavica* (black pudding) served with *žganci* (wheat, buckwheat or corn polenta), or *cmoki* (dumplings).

Being a tiny country, dishes on offer are much the same throughout, though it goes without saying that seafood is more abundant and more likely to be fresh (not frozen) on the coast, while the best trout is to be found in lakeside or riverside restaurants.

Where to Eat

To rub shoulders with the locals and experience something close to home cooking, eat at an informal *gostilna* (tavern) or *gostišče* (inn – these offer accommodation as well as food). The better ones are cosy, old-fashioned establishments, with rustic interiors and an informal atmosphere. The menu is usually limited, but the standard of the food is always reliable. At lunchtime many offer a bargain-priced fixed menu *(dnevno kosilo)*, consisting of three courses: soup, a main course and a side salad. If you chose to dine in a *restavracija* (restaurant) you will find the service and setting more formal, the menu more international, the prices higher, and the clientele largely made up of foreigners.

Over the border

Italians are often known to drive over the border into Slovenia for lunch or dinner, a mark of the high quality of the country's restaurants.

Enjoying alfresco drinks on a riverside promenade in Ljubljana

For the most authentic experience, try a *turistična kmetija* (agrotourism centre), where you are guaranteed top-notch home cooking using fresh, locally produced ingredients. Most serve such things as home-made wine, olive oil, cheese and sausages, along with fresh baked bread, and seasonal specialities such as *šparglji* (asparagus) in spring or *gobe* (mushrooms) and *radič* (radicchio) in autumn. The carefully restored old stone farmhouses set in rural surroundings are often worth the visit in themselves, and some offer overnight accommodation and countryside activities such as horse riding. For a comprehensive listing check out www.slovenia-tourism.si/touristfarms. Note that most agrotourism centres prefer you to telephone at least one day in advance so they can prepare for your arrival.

On a similar note, it is worth looking out for the new breed of 'Slow Food' establishments *(see page 101)*. These put an emphasis on old-fashioned recipes prepared from

Slow food, freshly prepared

superior local produce. Meals are served at a relaxed pace, generally consisting of eight courses or more, with a different wine to accompany each course.

Restaurants serving foreign dishes are sadly few and far between, except in Ljubljana, where you will find a number of Chinese and Mexican restaurants. The one universal dish that goes down well with everyone, especially children, is *pica* (pizza). Most towns and resorts have at least one pizzeria, often serving pizzas on a par with those across the border in Italy.

Last but not least, grills and snack bars, known as *bife* or *okrepčevalnica*, serve cheap and sometimes rather greasy Balkan favourites such as *pljeskavice* (burgers) and *čevapčiči* (meat croquettes), plus Balkan-style *burek* (filo-pastry pie filled with either cheese or minced meat).

When to Eat

Zajtrk (breakfast) in a hotel is usually a self-service cold buffet. The better ones offer yoghurt, cereal, fruit, meats, cheese, hard-boiled eggs, sausages, bread, butter, jam and honey. If your accommodation does not include breakfast, you can wake up over a cup of coffee in a café, though few offer a full breakfast menu. For pastries and cakes, track down a *slaščičarna* (cake shop).

Kosilo (lunch) is generally eaten between noon and 2pm. In some of the busier resorts, restaurants operate all afternoon.

Alternatively, if you are sightseeing you might prefer to make do with a snack *(see page 100)*, or if you are hiking you could pack a picnic.

Večerja (dinner) is normally eaten between 7pm and 10pm. However, there are no hard and fast rules: some restaurants along the coast stay open late in summer, while those in the mountains tend to close early all year round (in Bohinj most are shut by 10pm).

Note that most restaurants are closed one day a week, to give the staff a day off. In working cities such as Ljubljana, this will usually occur on Sunday (when many locals head out of town anyway), while in the resorts it is more likely to be on Monday.

Slow Food in Slovenia

The Slow Food movement was founded in 1986 as a reaction against fast food. When McDonald's opened an outlet next to the 18th-century Spanish Steps in Rome, many Italians were horrified at the thought of a modern eyesore so close to this splendid monument. As a result of their protests, McDonald's toned down the façade, but continued serving the burgers and chips. One of the protesters, journalist Carlo Petrini, gathered a group of left-wing intellectual friends and founded 'Slow Food'. Their manifesto called for a revival of people sitting down together round a table and indulging in the ancient ritual of eating. They also called for the reintroduction of regional recipes and the use of locally produced ingredients.

Slovenia joined in the movement in 1995, and is now home to several highly regarded Slow Food restaurants – look out for the snail symbol. In fact, Slovenia was spared the mass industrial production, food processing and supermarket standardisation that has overwhelmed many western countries, because of the decades spent in communist Yugoslavia.

What to Eat

Ljubljana offers a wide choice of restaurants, serving anything from Slovenian traditional dishes to stylish nouvelle fusion cuisine. There are also several surprisingly good seafood restaurants in the capital, with daily deliveries of fresh fish from the coast.

However, to enjoy the best seafood go down to one of the seaside towns in the southwest. Kick off with *hobotnica v solati* (octopus salad), *školjke* (mussels) or *rižota* (risotto), followed by fresh fish cooked *na žaru* (barbecued) – favourites include *brancin* (sea bass) and *orada* (gilthead bream) – accompanied by a colourful side salad and a bottle of local white Malvazija wine. While in the region, look out for seasonal specialities such as asparagus and artichokes in spring, and truffles in autumn.

Jota made from barley

Directly behind the coast, the Karst is renowned for *pršut* (air-dried ham, similar to Italian prosciutto), *jota* (a heavy soup made from beans, sauerkraut and barley) and the full-bodied red Teran wine. If you are travelling from Ljubljana down to the Karst area, en route you might like to stop in the former mining town of Idrija to try their delicious, old-fashioned *žlikrofi* (ravioli filled with potato and marjoram).

Traditional *potica*

Up in the northwest, the Soča Valley is much loved by fishermen and gourmets for its excellent *postrv* (wild trout), as is Lake Bohinj in Triglav National Park.

Once one ventures into the mountains the local food becomes heavier and simpler, with hearty peasant dishes consisting of basics such as cabbage, beans and potatoes, plus *klobasa* (sausage), *krvavica* (black pudding) and *žganci* (polenta). If you are lucky and it's in season, you might also find local game on the menu – *fazan* (pheasant), *medved* (bear), *srna* (venison) and *zajec* (rabbit) – and in autumn look out for *gobe* (mushrooms).

In the northeast and southeast, pork and poultry top the menu. Expect to see plenty of *zrezek* (pork cutlets), *salama* (salami) and *šunka* (ham), plus *puran* (turkey) and *gos* (goose). The closer you get to the Hungarian border, the more frequently you will find *golaž* (goulash) on offer.

Desserts

Standard desserts throughout the country include *palačinke* (pancakes, usually served with either walnuts, jam or chocolate), *sladoled* (ice cream), *potica* (rolled cake filled with walnuts or poppy seeds) and the ubiquitous *štruklji* (rolled dumpling, which can be either sweet or savoury).

Prekmurska gibanica is a scrumptious cake filled with layers of cream cheese, poppy seeds, walnuts and apple. It originates from the northeast, but if you are lucky you will also find it elsewhere on your travels.

What to Drink

Wine. Slovenia produces some top-quality wine *(vino)*, most of which is consumed within the country and never reaches the export market. Wines are certified according to their geographic origin (PGP). Those produced according to viticultural techniques specific to a particular region are labelled PTP.

Along the coast, be sure to try the white *(belo)* malvazija, which is an excellent accompaniment to seafood, and the red *(rdeče)* refošk, which goes well with meat dishes.

In the Karst region, the star is the robust red Teran, which is produced from the same grape as refošk, but here results in a significantly different wine due to the variation in both the soil and the climate.

In the northeast, semi-dry and semi-sweet whites predominate. Names to look out for are Renski rizling, Laški

Over 25 million gallons of wine are produced each year

rizling, Traminec, sauvignon, chardonnay, sivi pinot (pinot gris), beli pinot (pinot blanc), and the sparkling Penina.

In the southeast, the favourite tipple is *Cviček*, a light, sharp, rose-coloured wine, unique to Slovenia, which is produced from a blend of red and white grapes.

Unless you order a whole bottle, wine is served and priced by the decilitre (*deci*, one-tenth, is pronounced 'de-tsee'). A normal glass contains two *deci*.

Wine roads run through the three main producing regions

Beer *(pivo)* is served by the 0.5 litre or 0.3 litre. Ask for *veliko* (large) or *malo* (small) respectively. The two national favourite makes, Laško Zlatorog and Union, are both refreshing lagers which are served well chilled.

Spirits. Round off your meal with locally produced Slovenian spirits, *žganje*, made from distilled fruits. The most popular is the potent *slivovka*, made from plums, and the slightly tamer *viljamovka*, made from pears. *Medeno žganje* has been sweetened with honey.

Non-alcoholic drinks. *Mineralna voda* (mineral water) is drunk throughout the country, not because the tap water is bad, but for its health-giving properties. Slovenian *sok* (fruit juice) is famously tasty and wholesome, and goes down particularly well with children. If you go to a *kavarna* (café), order *kava* (coffee), which is usually served as a tiny cup of strong espresso, *kava s smetano* (with whipped cream), or *čaj* (tea), which is generally made from rose hips and served with lemon.

TO HELP YOU ORDER ...

Waiter/Waitress!	**Natakar/Gospodična, prosim!**
Could we have a table?	**Ali bi lahko dobili mizo?**
I'd like ...	**Rad(a) bi ...**
I'd like to pay.	**Rad(a) bi plačal(a).**

bread	**kruh**	pepper	**poper**
butter	**maslo**	potato	**krompir**
coffee	**kava**	rice	**riž**
fish dishes	**ribje jedi**	salad	**solata**
fruit	**sadje**	salt	**sol**
ice cream	**sladoled**	soup	**juha**
meat dishes	**mesne jedi**	sugar	**sladkor**
menu	**jedilnik**	tea	**čaj**
milk	**mleko**	wine	**vino**

Outdoor dining

... AND READ THE MENU

bakala	cod	**rižota**	risotto
burek	filo-pastry pie	**salama**	salami
fazan	pheasant	**sir**	cheese
golaž	goulash	**škampi**	shrimps
gos	goose	**školjke**	mussels
jetra	liver	**sladoled**	ice cream
klobasa	sausage	**smetana**	sour cream
krvavica	black pudding	**sok**	fruit juice
ligne	squid	**srna**	venison
medved	bear	**šunka**	ham (boiled)
njoki	gnocchi	**testenine**	pasta
palačinke	pancakes	**voda**	water
pivo	beer	**zajec**	rabbit
piščanec	chicken	**zavitek**	strudel
postrvi	trout	**žganci**	polenta
puran	turkey	**zrezek**	cutlet

SLOVENIAN SPECIALITIES

čevapčiči	meat rissoles
hobotnica v solati	octopus salad
jota	soup with beans, sauerkraut and barley
kranjska klobasa	firm, meaty sausage
ocvrti sir	cheese fried in breadcrumbs
potica	rolled cake with poppy seeds or walnuts
prekmurska gibanica	cake of cream cheese, poppy seeds, walnuts and apple
pršut	air-dried ham, like Italian prosciutto
sarma	cabbage rolls with rice and minced meat
štruklji	rolled dumpling (savoury or sweet)
žlikrofi	speciality from Idrija, similar to ravioli

PLACES TO EAT

We have used the following symbols to give an idea of the price for a three-course meal for one, excluding wine:

€€€€ over 30 euros **€€** 10–20 euros
€€€ 20–30 euros **€** below 10 euros

LJUBLJANA

AS €€€€ *Čopova 5a (off Knafljev prehod), tel: 01-425 88 22.* This outstanding restaurant, said to be the best in town, lies hidden away in a courtyard close to Wolfova ulica. The ambience is old-fashioned, with formal service, crisp white table linen and antique furniture, while the chef is noted for his excellent seafood and refined pasta dishes. Reservations recommended.

Julija €€€ *Stari trg 9, tel: 01-425 64 63.* This stylish but informal restaurant lies in the heart of the old town, with an interior decorated with ornate gilded mirrors. The cuisine is creative Mediterranean, with house specialities including octopus and rocket salad, and risotto with porcini mushrooms.

Ljubljanski dvor €€ *Dvorni trg 1, tel: 01-251 65 55.* With a beautiful open-air terrace close to Shoemaker's Bridge, Ljubljanski dvor offers a magnificent selection of thin-based pizzas, said by many to be the best in town.

Pri Škofu €€ *Rečna 8, Krakovo, tel: 01-426 45 08.* Much loved by both locals and visitors, this friendly restaurant has a daily changing menu. Expect Slovenian favourites such as octopus salad, gnocchi, risotto, and buckwheat *štruki* (dumplings) served in a colourful, Bohemian setting.

Ribica € *Tržnica (Central Market), no tel.* Inside Plečnik's riverside arcade, next to the covered fish market, Ribica serves great value-for-money seafood snacks such as fried squid, sardines and whitebait. Mon–Fri 7am–4pm, Sat 8am–2pm.

Špajza €€€ *Gornji trg 28, tel: 01-425 30 94.* A romantic and cosy retreat for dinner in the old town, Špajza serves creative Mediterranean dishes such as grilled mushrooms with gorgonzola and shrimp cream risotto in a series of candlelit rooms on the hill below the castle.

Zlata ribica €€ *Cankarjevo nabrežje 5, tel: 01-241 26 80.* This informal restaurant overlooking the river close to the Triple Bridge serves reasonably priced, Italian-cum-Slovenian favourites, with an emphasis on seafood. You might have to wait for a table on Sunday lunchtimes, when the place is packed with antiques hunters from the nearby flea market.

NORTHWEST

BLED

Mlino €€ *Cesta svobode 45, tel: 04-574 14 04.* A 20-minute walk along the lakeside from the centre brings you to this informal family restaurant with tables outside on a large terrace. Barbecued meats are the main pull, and there's a children's menu. From the landing station outside you can rent a rowing boat and explore the lake.

Pri Planincu €€ *Grajska 8, tel: 04-574 16 13.* Located above Lake Bled, on the road to the castle, this much-loved restaurant serves up hearty Slovenian food such as *klobasa* (sausage), *krvavica* (black pudding) and walnut *štruklji* (dumplings), plus pizza. At lunchtime, locals sit in the front room over beer and the fixed-price menu of the day.

Vila Prešeren €€€€ *Veslaška promenada 14, tel: 04-575 25 10.* Located in a white villa dating back to 1868, this used to be a holiday retreat for high-ranking officers in the Yugoslav National Army. The upmarket lakeside restaurant offers sophisticated dishes such as pasta with smoked salmon, and gilt-head bream filled with mushrooms. The dining room is quite formal, and there's a lovely summer terrace with views across the water to the island.

BOHINJ

Erlah €€ *Ukanc 67, tel: 04-572 33 09.* At the west end of the lake, near Hotel Zlatorog, on the way to Savica waterfall, Erlah serves fresh trout direct from a glass tank, as well as other local favourites. There are outdoor tables on the terrace in summer.

Gostilna Rupa €€€ *Srednja vas 87, tel: 04-572 34 01.* 5km (3 miles) from Ribčev Laz, this much-loved inn serves substantial portions of home cooking on a terrace with lovely views of the valley and mountains. House specialities include local trout, pork and venison. Occasional live music. Tue–Sun.

KOBARID

Topli Val €€€€ *Trg svobode 1, tel: 05-389 93 00.* On the ground floor of Hotel Hvala, this highly regarded restaurant offers some of the best seafood in the country, with daily deliveries direct from the coast, plus local river fish. Long-standing favourites include creamy prawn soup, shellfish prepared Dalmatian-style in olive oil and garlic, trout in fennel sauce and sea bass baked in a salt crust. The house dessert is *kobariški štruklji* (dumplings with walnut filling).

KRANJSKA GORA

Gostilna pri Martinu €€€ *Borovška 61, tel: 04-582 03 00.* This highly regarded, old-fashioned inn serves wholesome Slovenian favourites such as trout, venison, veal, home-made sausages and dumplings, all guaranteed to warm you up after a day's skiing.

RADOVLJICA

Gostilna Lectar €€€ *Linhartov trg 2, tel: 04-537 48 00.* Occupying a 16th-century building, Gostilna Lectar has been an inn since 1822. It serves local specialities such as pumpkin soup, buckwheat *štruklji* (dumplings) and apple strudel in a cosy, rustic dining room with a beamed ceiling and an open fire. In summer there are also tables outdoors in the garden. Wed–Sun.

SOUTHWEST

IDRIJA

Restauracija Barbara €€€ *Kosovelova 3, tel: 05-377 11 62.* The best place to try the local speciality, *žlikrofi* (potato balls flavoured with marjoram and wrapped in pasta), served here in a rich truffle sauce. Main courses include venison and wild boar, followed by a selection of home-made gateaux for dessert. The staff also arrange cooking and wine-tasting classes. The opening hours are a little unusual: Mon–Fri 4pm–10pm.

KOPER

Istrska klet Slavček € *Župančičeva 39, tel: 05-627 67 29.* In the heart of the old town, this tiny rustic wine bar serves home-made Istrian specialities such as *jota* (soup made from beans, sauerkraut and barley), *pršut* (air-dried ham similar to Italian prosciutto) and *ligne* (squid). Mon–Fri 6am–9pm.

Za gradom €€€ *Kraljeva 10, tel: 05-628 55 05.* 1.5km (1 mile) out of Koper, on Semedela hill, this highly successful Slow Food restaurant employs local, seasonal produce to create beautifully presented dishes such as home-made cheese ravioli, gnocchi with rocket, sea bass carpaccio, sole with truffles, and strawberries with green pepper. Tue–Sat. Reservations essential.

PIRAN

Ivo €€€ *Gregorčičeva 3, tel: 05-673 22 33.* Of the string of touristy seafood restaurants that line Piran's coastal promenade, unpretentious Ivo is one of the best. Try the grilled squid and barbecued sea bass, or for a bit of everything order the generous fish platter for two. The summer terrace has a memorable sea view.

Neptune €€€€ *Župančičeva 7, tel: 05-673 41 11.* Still the best restaurant in town according to locals, tiny Neptune serves Italian-inspired dishes such as gnocchi with shrimps and gorgonzola, plus quality fresh fish prepared over charcoal.

PORTOROÎ

Ribič €€€ *Seča, tel: 05-677 07 90.* Most of Portorož's restaurants are impersonal establishments attached to hotels lining the seafront promenade. But Ribič, 1.5km (1 mile) out of town on the way to the Sečovlje saltpans, has its own garden terrace giving onto the sea. This seafood restaurant, serving excellent mussels, shrimps and barbecued fresh fish, plus good local wines.

NORTHEAST

IVANJKOVCI

Taverna €€€ *Veličane 59, tel: 02-719 41 28.* A perfect spot for lunch in the Jeruzalem Wine Road area, this well-established restaurant serves roast meats and fresh trout. In summer, the outdoor tables offer photogenic views over the vineyards on the surrounding hills. You can also ask to taste the wines in the stone cellar below.

MARIBOR

Toti rotovž €€€ *Glavni trg 14, tel: 02-228 76 50.* On the main square, next door to the 16th-century Town Hall, Toti rotovž serves classic Slovenian fare on the ground floor, and delicious barbecued steaks in the atmospheric, vaulted brick cellars below.

PTUJ

Gostilna Perutnina €€ *Novi trg 2, tel: 02-749 06 22.* Located in the centre of town, this restaurant is famed for its excellent chicken dishes, with house specialities including chicken in breadcrumbs, chicken livers with buckwheat *kaša*, and a chicken salad platter. They also do a bargain buffet brunch daily. There's a large summer terrace out front. Mon–Sat 9am–7pm, Sun noon–4pm.

Ribič €€€ *Dravska ulica 9, tel: 02-749 06 35.* Ribič serves freshwater fish specialities like *ribje brodet* (fish stew) and *postrv* (trout). Throughout the summer, guests dine on an open-air terrace that looks over the river. Tue–Sat.

SOUTHEAST

ČATEŽ

Gostilna ob sotočju €€€ *Zagrebška cesta 9, tel: 07-499 04 50.* This long-standing eatery serves a good selection of Slovenian meat and fish dishes, with house specialities including marinated pork fillet and veal medallions. Be sure to try the locally produced *cviček* wine. They also offer wine tasting in a nearby vineyard cottage by appointment. Lunch and dinner Mon–Sat.

MOKRICE

Mokrice Castle Hotel Restaurant €€€€ *Rajec 4, tel: 07-457 42 40.* This exclusive restaurant occupies one of the corner turrets of Mokrice Castle Hotel. The menu features beautifully presented hearty Slovenian dishes including first class game and freshwater fish, plus an excellent wine list.

NOVO MESTO

Janez Kos Restaurant €€ *Šmarješka cesta 26, tel: 07-337 05 40.* Overlooking the River Krka on the edge of town, this friendly eatery serves a decent range of regional cuisine with several dishes suitable for vegetarians. Wine tasting is also offered in the stone cellar of a nearby cottage by appointment. Lunch and dinner Mon–Sat.

OTOČEC

Šeruga €€ *Sela pri Ratežu, tel: 07-334 69 00.* This popular family-run agrotourism centre, in a complex of traditional farm buildings, lies 4km (2½ miles) from Otočec Castle. The menu includes rabbit, trout, rural dishes like *štruklji* (dumplings) and *potica* (cake rolls filled with walnuts or poppy seeds), plus the family's homemade *cviček* wine.

A–Z TRAVEL TIPS

A Summary of Practical Information

A

ACCOMMODATION (see also CAMPING, YOUTH HOSTELS and the list of RECOMMENDED HOTELS on page 136)

Hotels. Since independence, many hotels that were formerly aimed at the package-tourism market have been upgraded to provide luxurious extras, such as 'wellness centres' and business facilities. Several small, family-run hotels have also entered the market.

Hotels are graded by the Slovenian Tourist Board: one- and two-star establishments are rather basic; three-star hotels are comfortable and offer decent service; and four- and five-star hotels are plush and have a range of extra amenities. The most upmarket hotels are found in the popular resorts of Portorož on the coast and Bled on the edge of Triglav National Park. There are also a couple of high-class, atmospheric castle-hotels at Otočec and Mokrice

Note that prices shoot up during high season (July–Aug along the coast, and Christmas and New Year in the ski resorts), and that many hotels offer better rates for stays of more than three days.

Private accommodation. In the areas that attract tourists, such as the coast, Bled and Bohinj, private accommodation is reasonably priced and of a high standard, ranging from rooms with shared bathrooms to self-catering apartments. Some but not all of the local Tourist Information Centres (TICs) can help you find private accommodation; if a TIC cannot help, try local travel agencies.

I'd like a ... room ...	**Rad(a) bi ... sobo ...**	*rat (raada) bi **so**bo*
single	**enoposteljno**	*eno**poh**stelno*
double	**dvoposteljno**	*dvo**poh**stelno*
with a bath	**s kopalno kadjo**	*s ko**paa**lno ka**dyoh***
with a shower	**s prho**	*s **perr**ho*
What's the rate per night?	**Koliko stane na noč?**	***koh**liko **staa**ne na nohch*

Tourist farms. To gain real insight into rural life in Slovenia, stay at a *turistična kmetija* (agrotourism centre). Ideal for families with children, a stay on a working farm offers direct contact with nature. Most are set in peaceful, unspoilt countryside, and provide authentic home cooking made from local seasonal produce. For further information visit www.slovenia.info.

AIRPORTS

Ljubljana international airport (tel: 04-206 19 81, www.lju-airport.si) is 23km (14 miles) from the city centre. Monday to Friday there is an hourly bus service to the city centre; at weekends this is reduced to every two hours; the last departure from the airport is around 8pm. The journey takes 45 minutes, and tickets (€4.10) can be purchased on the bus. The same journey by taxi costs around €40.

There is a small international airport at **Maribor**. **Trieste** airport in Italy is another option, particularly for the coast. In Austria, regular trains run from **Graz** to Maribor, and **Klagenfurt** can be good if you are hiring a car.

What bus do I take for the town centre?	**Kateri avtobus pelje v center mesta?**	*katehri awtobus pehlye oo tsenterr mehsta*
How much is the fare to ...?	**Koliko stane do ...?**	*kohliko staane do*

B

BICYCLE HIRE

Cycling is popular in sporting, ecologically-minded Slovenia. Ljubljana has a new self-service bicycle hire scheme with 30 docking stations (www.bicikelj.si), and the Ljubljana Tourist Information Centre (TIC) hires bicycles. In Ljubljana and Maribor many locals travel on two wheels, and the city centres have bike lanes. Bicycles are available for hire in any part of the country where you would conceivably want to ride one, most notably in Triglav National Park, where several agencies also organise cycling tours.

BUDGETING FOR YOUR TRIP

Still reasonably cheap by Western standards, prices in Slovenia are far higher than those in former Eastern Bloc countries such as the Czech Republic and Hungary.

Accommodation. A standard double room with en-suite bath and breakfast in a five-star hotel costs around €180 a night, while prices for a double in a three-star hotel range from €60–80.

Meals. A three-course meal for two with a bottle of wine in a decent restaurant costs around €50. A set-menu lunch *(dnevno kosilo)* in a no-frills *gostilna* costs around €10 per person.

Drinks. Alcoholic drinks are reasonably priced, with a bottle of local beer costing around €2 in a down-to-earth *gostilna* (tavern), and a glass of decent wine in a *vinoteke* (wine bar) €3.

Entertainment. A cinema or local chamber concert ticket is around €5, and a full orchestral concert will be from €5–35.

Public transport. Trains and buses are inexpensive. City bus fares are around €1. Taxi and minibus transfers are around €1 per km.

Car hire. A week's car hire costs upwards of €300, depending on the model and the type of insurance. Petrol is around €1.25 a litre.

C

CAMPING

Slovenia has more than 30 small, well-equipped campsites. Most are along the coast and in the mountains, and are open May to September. The best are said to be Zlatorog by Lake Bohinj and Camping Bled by Lake Bled. Ljubljana Resort is 4km (2½ miles) north of the city centre in Ježica on the banks of the River Sava.

Two campsites cater for naturists: Camp Smlednik by Lake Zbilje, 20km (13 miles) north of Ljubljana on the way to Kranj, and Banovci Spa in Veržej in the northeast of the country.

Camping outside organised campsites is not permitted. For further information visit www.slovenia.info.

CAR HIRE (see also DRIVING and BUDGETING FOR YOUR TRIP)

International and local car-hire companies operate from Ljubljana Airport and in all the main towns and resorts. Some companies allow one-way rentals to Croatia and Bosnia. To hire a car, you must be 21 or over and hold a valid driving licence. Bookings for major companies can be made online:

Avantcar www.avantcar-slovenia.com
Avis www.avis.si
Budget www.budget.si
Europcar www.europcar.si
Hertz www.hertz.si
Sixt www.si.sixt.com

I'd like to hire a car.	**Rad(a) bi najel(a) avto.**	*rat (**raa**da) bi nay**ehw aaw**to*
I'd like it for a day/ a week.	**Za en dan/ teden.**	*za en daan/ **teh**den*
What's the charge per day/week?	**Koliko stane na dan/teden?**	***koh**liko **staa**ne na daan/**teh**den*

CLIMATE

Slovenia has three distinct climatic regions. The mountains have an Alpine climate with warm summers and cold winters with heavy snow; the coast has a Mediterranean climate with hot, sunny summers and mild winters; and the inland region has a Continental climate with hot, dry summers and icy winters. Generally, the best periods to visit are

May–June or Sept–Oct, when you can expect dry, warm weather, ideal for outdoor sports such as hiking and mountain biking. Try to avoid July and August, when temperatures can rise above 30°C (86°F) and tourist destinations are horribly busy, especially on the coast. In the ski season (Dec–Mar) temperatures can drop as low as –20°C (–4°F) in the mountains. Average temperatures in Ljubljana are:

	J	F	M	A	M	J	J	A	S	O	N	D
Max °C	2	5	10	15	20	24	27	26	22	15	8	4
Min °C	–4	–4	0	4	9	12	14	14	11	6	2	–1
Max °F	36	41	50	59	68	75	81	79	72	59	46	39
Min °F	25	25	32	39	48	54	57	57	52	43	36	30

CLOTHING

Take light cotton clothes, sunglasses and sunscreen in summer; plenty of jumpers, a warm coat, hat and gloves in winter. Be sure to pack comfortable walking shoes for sightseeing, as most historic towns have steep, cobbled streets. Bring sports clothes for outdoor activities such as hiking and biking. Pack casual-chic for Ljubljana and the coastal resorts, where you might wish to dress up at night.

CRIME AND SAFETY (see also EMERGENCIES and POLICE)

Slovenia is safe by any Western European standards. Nonetheless, visitors should take the usual precautions of keeping valuables in a safe place. To report a crime, call the police, tel: **113**.

I want to report a theft.	**Prijavil(a) bi krajo.**	*priy**aa**viw (priy**aa**vila) bi **kraa**yo*
Call the police.	**Pokličite policijo.**	*po**klee**chite poli**tsee**yo*
Stop thief!	**Ustavite tatu!**	*ust**aa**vite ta**too***
Help!	**Na pomoč!**	*na po**mohch***

D

DRIVING (see also GETTING THERE BY CAR)

Rules and regulations. Slovenes drive on the right-hand side of the road. The speed limits are 50km/h (31mph) in residential areas, 90km/h (56mph) on local roads, 100km/h (63mph) on highways, and 130km/h (81mph) on motorways. The police are notoriously tough on those caught speeding (fines are heavy) or drinking-and-driving (0.5g of alcohol per kg of blood is the limit). If you are caught using a mobile phone without a hands-free device while driving you also risk a stiff fine. Remember that seatbelts must be worn in both the front and the back of the car, and children under 12 are not allowed to sit in the front. Headlights must be switched on *at all times*, even during the day.

Roads. These vary from the slick new motorways to mountain roads, some of which are closed in winter, notably the Vršič Pass. The motorway network is being extended and upgraded. Motorways are subject to toll charges. It is generally cheaper to buy a weekly or monthly vignette *(vinjeta)*, available at the borders and at most large petrol stations. This must be displayed when travelling on motorways. Also, there is a toll for the Karavanke Tunnel (between Slovenia and Austria).

The Automobile Association of Slovenia (tel: 1987; www.amzs.si) provides a 24-hour rescue service.

cona za pešce	pedestrian zone
delo na cesti	road works
enosmerna ulica	one way
izvoz	exit (motorway)
nevarnost	danger
obvoz	detour
parkirni prostor	parking zone

E

ELECTRICITY

The standard electric current is 220V, 50Hz. Plugs have two round pins. Visitors from the UK and the US will need an adaptor for electrical appliances such as razors and hair dryers.

EMBASSIES AND CONSULATES

Embassies and consulates based in Ljubljana:

Australian Consulate Železna Cesta 14, tel: 01-234 88 75.

Canadian Consulate Trg Republike 3, tel: 01-252 44 44.

Irish Embassy Poljanski nasip 6, tel: 01-300 89 70; www.embassyofireland.si.

New Zealand Consulate Verovškova 57, tel: 01-580 30 55.

UK Embassy Trg Republike 3/IV, tel: 01-200 39 10; www.ukinslovenia.fco.gov.uk

US Embassy Prešernova cesta 31, tel: 01-200 55 00; www.slovenia.usembassy.gov.

embassy	**veleposlaništvo**	*veleposlaanishtvo*

EMERGENCIES (see also HEALTH AND MEDICAL CARE)

Police	**113**
Fire Brigade	**112**
Ambulance	**112**

There's been an accident.	**Zgodila se je nesreča.**	*zgodeela se ye nesrehcha*
Call a doctor/ an ambulance quickly.	**Hitro pokličite zdravnika/ rešilni avto.**	*heetro pokleechite zdrawneeka/ resheelni aawto*

G

GAY AND LESBIAN TRAVELLERS

Regarding homosexuality, Slovenia is certainly the most tolerant of the former Yugoslav countries, though it remains less open to public displays of affection than Western Europe. The capital held its first Gay Pride, Ljubljana Pride (www.ljubljanapride.org), in 2001, and this has become an annual one-week event. The website www.sloveniaforgaytravelers.com has a 'Gay Guide to Slovenia' listing haunts popular with gays and lesbians, offers tours, and has a useful page of links to other sites.

GETTING THERE (see also AIRPORTS)

By Air. National carriers offering regular flights to Ljubljana include Adria Airways, Air France, Austrian Airlines, ČSA Czech Airlines, JAT Airways, LOT, Malev, and Turkish Airlines.

Slovenia's national carrier is Adria Airways (Gospodvetska 6, Ljubljana, tel: 01-239 19 10; www.adria.si; ticketing agent at London Gatwick, tel: 01293 507 182). It offers regular scheduled flights to Ljubljana from London Gatwick (journey time 2 hours) and Manchester, and many other major European cities.

Low-cost carrier easyJet (www.easyjet.com) offers frequent flights from London Stansted to Ljubljana. Adria Airways, the national carrier, sometimes offers good-value deals. Ryanair (www.ryanair.com) flies from London Stansted and Birmingham to Trieste in Italy, from where Slovenia can be reached by car (by bus or train is slow). Ryanair also flies from London Stansted to Klagenfurt and Graz in Austria, both near the border, with Graz having regular trains to Maribor.

There are no direct flights to Slovenia from outside Europe. Adria operates with Lufthansa to provide indirect flights from the US via Germany. Air France and Delta operate via Paris.

By Rail. Direct trains run to Slovenia from Italy, Austria, Hungary, Croatia, Serbia and Germany. There are speedy Eurocity services to

Ljubljana from Zagreb (journey time 2hrs 15min), Venice (4hrs), Vienna (4hrs 10min) and Munich (6hrs 20min).

Inter-rail one-country passes for Slovenia (www.raileurope.co.uk) are relatively inexpensive, but while the rail network is good, it is limited in where it goes and buses are often a better option.

For national and international information, contact Ljubljana train station: Kolodvorska 11, tel: 01-291 33 32; www.slo-zeleznice.si.

By Bus. Buses run to Slovenia from all its neighbouring countries. If you are departing from the UK, Eurolines (www.eurolines.com) operate a bus service from London Victoria to Ljubljana (journey time approx 28hrs) with a change in Frankfurt, Germany.

For national and international bus information, contact Ljubljana Bus Station: Trg OF 4, 1000 Ljubljana, tel: 1991 (from a Slovenian phone); www.ap-ljubljana.si.

By Car. There are motorways leading into Slovenia from neighbouring Italy, Austria, Hungary and Croatia. Foreign vehicles from outside the EU require an International Green Card to enter Slovenia, which can be purchased at the border.

GUIDES AND TOURS

The travel agency **Kompas** (www.kompas.net) offers guided coach tours of Slovenia, such as a seven-day 'Highlights of Slovenia'.

In the capital, Ljubljana Tourist Information Centre (TIC) (Adamic-Lundrovo nabrezje 2, near Tromostovje, tel: 01-306 12 15; www.visitljubljana.si) offers the following scheduled tours of Ljubljana, departing daily at fixed times from the square in front of the Town Hall, all priced at €10 (€5 children under 12) and lasting about 2 hours: Walking tour and funicular ride (Apr–Oct 10am, Oct–Mar 11am); Walking tour and tourist train ride (Apr–Oct 5pm); Walking tour and boat ride (Apr–Oct 2pm); Boat tour to the Botanic Garden (June–Sept Sat only, 4pm). Special rates are available for groups.

The Ljubljana TIC also offers guided tours of Ljubljana by arrangement, and can help arrange excursions outside Ljubljana –

such as to the Postojna Caves, Bled, Alpine scenery or vineyards.

In other towns of historical interest, enquire at the local Tourist Information Centre (TIC) for guided tours.

Also note that Lipica Stud Farm, Škocjan Caves and Postojna Cave can be visited only as part of scheduled guided tours.

Is there an English-speaking guide?	**Ali kakšen vodnik govori angleško?**	*aali **kak**shen vod**neek** govo**ree** **anglehshko***

H

HEALTH AND MEDICAL CARE

There are no specific health risks in Slovenia and the water is safe to drink throughout the country. As in much of Central Europe, if you get flu-like symptoms after a tick bite, see a doctor immediately because of the risk of encephalitis. In an emergency telephone **112** for an ambulance.

Members of the EU countries are entitled to free emergency medical treatment providing they have a European Health Insurance Card (EHIC), which can be obtained at post offices or online at www.ehic.org.uk.

24-hour pharmacies in major towns:
Ljubljana: Prisojna ulica 7, tel: 01-230 62 30.
Maribor: Glavni trg 20, tel: 02-229 47 40.
Kranj: Bleiweisova 8, tel: 04-201 61 34.
Novo mesto: Kandijski cesta 1, tel: 07-393 29 18.

L

LANGUAGE

Slovenian is a South Slavic language written in Latin script. Fortunately for foreign visitors, most young people speak good English, plus either Italian or German. Older people are more likely to speak Italian as a second language along the coast, and German as a second language in the northeast. Note that on the coast, many places have two names, both Slovenian and Italian, which can be confusing: for example Koper is also known as Capodistria, and Piran as Pirano.

Pronunciation of most letters is roughly like that in English. However, 'c' is pronounced as 'ts', 'j' as 'y', and in certain words 'v' as if it were 'u'. Accented characters are 'č' as 'ch', 'š' as 'sh', and 'ž', something like the 'ge' in 'orange'.

The following are some useful words and phrases in Slovenian:

yes	**ja**	*ya*
no	**ne**	*ne*
please	**prosim**	**proh***sim*
thank you	**hvala**	**hvaa***la*
good morning	**dobro jutro**	*dobro* **yoo***tro*
good afternoon	**dober dan**	**doh***ber* **daan**
good evening	**dober večer**	**doh***ber ve***chehr**
good-bye	**na svidenje**	*na* **sveed***enye*
excuse me/sorry	**oprostite**	*opro***steete**
Where?	**Kje/Kam?**	*kyeh/kaam*
When?	**Kdaj?**	*kdaay*
How long?	**Kako dolgo?**	*ka***koh dow***go*
How far?	**Kako daleč?**	*ka***koh daa***lech*
left	**levo**	**leh***vo*
right	**desno**	**deh***sno*
open	**odprt**	*od***perrt**
closed	**zaprt**	*za***perrt**
old	**star**	*staar*
new	**nov**	*now*
early	**zgoden**	**zgoh***den*
late	**pozen**	**po***zen*

M

MAPS

The Slovenian Tourist Board publishes an excellent *Tourist Map of Slovenia*, available free from the head office or through the website. In addition, most local Tourist Information Centres can supply visitors with city or regional maps, or if they are in rural areas with maps of local hiking routes.

MEDIA

The Slovenian media world is relatively free and unbiased.

The most popular national newspapers are *Dnevnik* and *Delo* (both Ljubljana-based dailies), *Večer* (a Maribor-based daily) and *Primorske Novice* (a Koper-based daily). The top-selling magazine is *Mladina*, which was founded in 1943 as a youth publication, but played a major role in Slovenia's drive for independence from Yugoslavia, when its editor was put on trial. It continues today as a highly respected political and lifestyle weekly.

Locally based, English-language publications to look out for are the fortnightly *Slovenia Times*, a newspaper aimed primarily at foreign businesspeople and diplomats, and *Ljubljana Life*, a bimonthly magazine listing bars, restaurants and entertainment in the capital. In addition, foreign-language newspapers and magazines are readily available in Ljubljana and in the busier resorts.

Slovenia has two state-run television channels operated by RTV Slovenia, plus the privately owned stations Pop TV and Kanal A. Films are shown in original version with subtitles. About two-thirds of TV households are connected to cable or satellite TV, and most hotel rooms are also equipped with satellite TV.

MONEY (see also BUDGETING FOR YOUR TRIP)

The Slovenian Tolar (SIT), introduced at independence in 1991, was replaced by the Euro (€) on 1 January 2007.

Visitors can change foreign currency in banks, post offices and some of the larger hotels. Most banks, even in small provincial towns, have ATMs, and the larger hotels, restaurants and shops accept credit cards.

I want to change some dollars/pounds.	**Zamenjal(a) bi nekaj dolarjev/funtov.**	*za**meh**nyaw (za**meh**nyala) bi **neh**kay **doh**laryerw/**foon**tow*
What's the exchange rate?	**Kakšen je menjalni tečaj?**	***kack**shen ye menyaalni te**chaay***
Can you change these traveller's cheques?	**Ali lahko unovčite te potovalne čeke?**	***aa**li lah**koh** wnowhchite te poto**vaa**lne **cheh**ke*

O

OPENING TIMES

Banks. Mon–Fri 9am–5pm, Sat 8am–noon.
Shops. Mon–Fri 8am–7pm, Sat 8am–1pm. Shops selling essential goods are allowed to open on Sundays and public holidays, but Sunday trading has been opposed by the Retail Workers Trade Union.
Markets. Most larger towns stage an open-air fruit-and-vegetable market Mon–Sat 7am–2pm.
Museums. The larger museums are generally open Tue–Sun 10am–6pm during summer, with reduced hours in winter. Some of the smaller museums are shut completely through winter.
Petrol Stations. 7am–8pm Mon–Sat; major stations open 24 hours.

P

POLICE (see also EMERGENCIES)

The police *(policija)* are generally helpful and friendly, though their presence at border crossings can seem intimidating. Slovenia is now part of the Schengen Agreement (which removes passports and customs controls at borders between signatory states), and is therefore under pressure from other EU countries to demonstrate that its borders with non-EU countries are strictly controlled.

Tickets issued by police for motoring offences are payable at banks and post offices.

Where's the lost property office/ police station?	**Kje je urad za najdene predmete/ policijska postaja?**	*kyeh ye uraat za **naay**dene pre**dmeh**te poli**tseey**ska pos**taa**ya*
... has been stolen.	**Ukradli so mi ...**	*u**kraad**li so mi*
my wallet	**denarnico**	*de**naar**nitso*
my handbag	**torbico**	***tohr**bitso*
my passport	**potni list**	***pot**ni leest*

POST OFFICES

The postal service is operated by national Pošta Slovenije. Post offices in larger towns are open Mon–Fri 8am–7pm and Sat 8am–1pm; those in smaller towns and villages Mon–Fri 8am–2pm and Sat 8am–11am.

The exception is the post office at Trg OF in Ljubljana, next to the train station, which is open Mon–Fri 7am–midnight, Sat 7am–6pm and Sun 9am–noon, and the post office at Cegaletova 5, which is open 24 hours.

I want to send this by ...	**To bi rad(a) poslal(a) ...**	*toh bi rat (**raa**da) pos**laaw** (pos**laa**la)*
airmail	**z letalsko pošto**	*z le**taal**sko **pohsh**to*
express	**nujno**	***nooy**no*
registered	**priporočeno**	*priporo**che**no*
stamps	**znamke**	***znaam**ke*

PUBLIC HOLIDAYS

1–2 Jan	New Year holidays	*novo leto*
8 Feb	Slovenian Cultural Holiday	*slovenski kulturni praznik*
27 Apr	Resistance Day	*dan upora proti okupatorju*
1–2 May	Labour Day holidays	*praznik dela*
25 June	Slovenia Day	*dan državnosti*
15 Aug	Assumption Day	*veliki šmaren (Marijino vnebovzetje)*
31 Oct	Reformation Day	*dan reformacije*
1 Nov	All Saints' Day	*dan spomina na mrtve*
25 Dec	Christmas Day	*božič*
26 Dec	Independence Day	*dan samostojnosti*

Movable dates:

	Easter	*velika noč*
	Easter Monday	*velikonočni ponedeljek*

R

RELIGION

The return to independence brought a renewed affirmation of the Church. Monasteries are fully functioning and Sundays are duly respected. The majority (approximately 75 percent) are Roman Catholic. Alojz Uran was appointed Archbishop of Ljubljana in 2004. A second archdiocese was created in Maribor by Pope Benedict XVI in 2006.

The rest of the population are: 2.5 percent Orthodox Christian (mainly originating from Serbia, Montenegro, Macedonia and Bosnia), 1.5 percent Muslim (former immigrants from Bosnia and Herzegovina) and 1 percent Protestant (mostly in the northeast, close to the border with Hungary). The remaining 20 percent are either undecided or atheist.

T

TELEPHONES

The country code for Slovenia is 386. When calling from outside Slovenia, the first 0 in the area code is dropped. When dialling within Slovenia, the area code is dialled in full unless you are making the call from within that area. City area telphone codes are 1 (Ljubljana), 2 (Maribor), 4 (Kranj), 5 (Portorož), 7 (Novo mesto).

Public telephones on the street work with a phonecard (*telefonska kartica*), available from post offices and most newspaper kiosks. Calls can also be made from telephone cabins inside some but not all post offices. Calls made from hotel rooms work out to be very expensive.

The three Slovenian mobile phone networks (Mobitel, Si.mobil and Tušmobil) operate on the 900 and 1800 MHz bands. North American and some South American phones need to be tri-band. Phones from most of the rest of the world, including Europe, should be dual-band. SIM cards and phones are readily available from phone retailers in larger towns.

International directory enquiries: 989
Local directory enquiries: 988

TIME ZONES

Slovenia is one hour ahead of GMT and adopts daylight-saving time in summer:

New York	London	**Ljubljana**	Jo'burg	Sydney	Auckland
6am	11am	**noon**	noon	8pm	10pm

TIPPING

If you have enjoyed your meal and thought the service was good, it is usual to leave a tip of around 10 percent in restaurants. However, tipping in general is not the custom in Slovenia

TOILETS

There are few public toilets other than those found in train and bus stations, where it is usual to pay a small sum. Otherwise, you can always go into a café or bar to use their amenities, though in this case it is polite either to ask first, or to buy a quick drink. Generally, toilets, like everything else in Slovenia are remarkably clean.

Where are the toilets? **Kje je stranišče?** *kyeh ye stra**neesh**che*

TOURIST INFORMATION

The **Slovenian Tourist Board** runs a useful website at www.slovenia.info. There is a Slovenian Tourist Information Centre in Ljubljana at Krekov trg 10, tel: 01-306 45 75.

In the UK: Embassy of the Republic of Slovenia, 10 Little College Street, London SW1P 3SH, tel: 020-7222 5700.

There are also Slovenian tourist offices in Brussels, Milan, Munich and Vienna, but there are no offices outside Europe.

In Slovenia, most towns and even some villages have their own Tourist Information Centre (TIC). Some are listed below:

Ljubljana: Adamic-Lundrovo nabrezje 2, near Tromostovje, tel: 01-306 12 15; www.visitljubljana.si. There are also small TICs in the train station and at the airport.

Northwest

Bled: Cesta svobode 10, tel: 04-574 11 22; www.bled.si.
Bohinj: Ribčev Laz 48, tel: 04-574 60 10; www.bohinj.si.
Bovec: Trg golobarskih žrtev 8, tel: 05-384 19 19; www.bovec.si.
Kamnik: Glavni trg 2, tel: 01-831 82 50; www.kamnik-tourism.si.
Kobarid: Trg svobode 16, tel: 05-386 04 90; www.doline-soce.si.
Kranj: Koroška cesta 29, tel: 04-236 30 30; www.turisticnodrustvo-kranj.si.

Kranjska Gora: Tičarjeva 2, tel: 04-580 94 90; www.kranjska-gora.si.
Radovljica: Gorenjska cesta 1, tel: 04-531 53 00.
Škofja Loka: Mestni trg 7, tel: 04-512 02 68; www.skofjaloka.si.

Southwest
Idrija: Vodnikova 3, tel: 05-374 39 16; www.idrija-turizem.si.
Izola: Sončno nabrežje 4, tel: 05-640 10 50; www.izola.eu.
Koper: Titov trg 3, tel: 05-664 64 03; www.koper.si.
Nova Gorica: Bevkov trg 4, tel: 05-330 46 00; www.novagorica-turizem.com.
Piran: Tartinijev trg 2, tel: 05-673 44 40; www.portoroz.si.
Portorož: Obala 16, tel: 05-674 22 20; www.portoroz.si.
Postojna Cave: Jamska cesta 9, tel: 05-720 16 10; www.postojna-cave.com.
Štanjel: Štanjel 42, tel: 05-769 00 56; www.kras-carso.com.

Northeast
Celje: Krekov trg 3, tel: 03-428 79 36.
Ljutomer: Jureša Cirila 4, tel: 02-584 83 33; www.jeruzalem.si.
Logarska Dolina: Logarska dolina 9, tel: 03-838 90 04; www.logarska-dolina.si.
Maribor: Partizanska cesta 6a, tel: 02-234 66 11; www.maribor-pohorje.si.
Murska Sobota: Zvezna ulica 10, tel: 02-534 11 30; www.murska-sobota.si.
Ptuj: Slovensk i trg 5, tel: 02-779 60 11; www.ptuj-tourism.si.
Rogaška Slatina: Zdraviliški trg 1, tel: 03-581 44 14; www.rogaska-slatina.si.

Southeast
Dolenjske Toplice: Zdraviliški trg 8, tel: 07-384 51 88.
Novo mesto: Glavni trg 6, tel: 07-393 92 63; www.novomesto.si.

TRANSPORT

It is easy to get around Slovenia on public transport. Most places are within two hours of Ljubljana, so there is no overnight travel involved.

How much is the fare to ...?	**Koliko stane vozovnica do ...?**	*kohliko staane vozownitsa do*
I'd like a ticket to ... please.	**Vozovnico do ... prosim.**	*vozownitso do prahsim*
single (one-way)	**enosmerno**	*enosmehrno*
return (round trip)	**povratno**	*povraatno*

Buses. Buses are cheap and efficient, and the network is more extensive than the railways, which is why locals generally prefer buses to trains. In fact, you can reach almost anywhere in the country by bus, though some journeys may involve several changes.

Ljubljana Bus Station, tel: 1991 (from a Slovenian phone); www.ap-ljubljana.si.

Maribor Bus Station, tel: 02-235 02 12; www.veolia-transport.si.

Koper Bus Station, tel: 05-639 52 69.

Trains. Trains are cheap and comfortable, though due to the mountainous nature of the country the railways are less far-reaching than the bus network. The fastest and most frequent city services run from Ljubljana to Maribor, and Ljubljana to Koper.

Where can I get a taxi?	**Kje lahko dobim taksi?**	*kyeh lahkoh dobeem taaksi*
What's the fare to ...?	**Koliko stane do ...?**	*kohliko staane do*
Take me to ...	**Peljite me ...**	*pelyeete me*
this address	**na ta naslov**	*na taa naslow*
Please stop here.	**Tukaj ustavite, prosim.**	*tookay ustaavite prohsim*

Ljubljana Train Station, tel: 01-291 33 32; www.slo-zeleznice.si. Maribor Train Station, tel: 02-292 21 00. Koper Train Station, tel: 05-639 52 63. Worth a special mention are old-fashioned **steam trains** that operate on several lines during the tourist season. For information, visit www.slo-zeleznice.si, click on 'On the Trip', then the link 'Steam Train'.

Taxis. Taxis are available in all major towns but are by no means cheap. It's best to try to negotiate a fare before starting a journey.

V

VISAS AND ENTRY REQUIREMENTS

Most foreign visitors need a valid passport to enter Slovenia, though citizens of EU countries and Switzerland can enter the country with just a personal identity card for stays of up to 30 days. For stays of up to 90 days, citizens of EU countries, plus Norway, Iceland, Liechtenstein, the US, Canada and Australia can enter Slovenia without visas. South African nationals require visas.

Slovenia is a Schengen Agreement country so there are few controls at the borders with Austria and Italy.

Visitors from other nations should either visit the website www.mzz.gov.si (in Slovenian only) or check with the Slovenian embassy in their own country before arranging their trip.

Customs allowances are the same as for other EU countries. Note that when returning from Slovenia to the UK, goods must be for personal use or a gift (you may not receive any reimbursement).

W

WEBSITES AND INTERNET ACCESS

Slovenia is an internet-friendly country. Visitors should have no trouble finding an internet café in any of the larger towns and tourist destinations, and these are usually open from around 10am to

10pm. Many larger hotels also have internet corners and facilities.
www.slovenia.info The best general website is run by the Slovenian Tourist Board and offering extensive and up-to-date coverage of accommodation, transport and activities within the country.
www.sloveniatimes.com An English-language fortnightly newspaper featuring sports, culture, lifestyle and events.
www.uvi.si The government's public relations and media website, which files English language press releases about the country.
www.ljubljanalife.com An online magazine with cultural events.

Can I check my email?	**Ali lahko pogledam svojo elektronsko pošto?**	*aali lahkoh poglehdam svoyo elektrohnsko pohshto*

Y

YOUTH HOSTELS

There are some 25 youth hostels in Slovenia (see www.youth-hostel.si), seven of which are recognised by Hostelling International (www.hihostels.com): Črnomelj, Koper, Kranjska Gora, Ljubljana, Maribor, Podčetrtek and Portorož.

Most are open all year round, though some operate only in the summer. Reservations are recommended, especially in July and August. Expect to pay around €10 per person.

The one youth hostel worth a particular mention is **Celica** (Metelkova 8, www.souhostel.com; *see page 136*) in Ljubljana. The building was constructed in the 19th century as a military prison. Then, in 2003, artists and architects from all over Europe were invited to redesign the cells, to provide 20 two-bed rooms and dormitories. The result was such a success that non-residents can view the interior as part of a guided tour, daily at 2pm. With such a reputation, it is of course essential to book.

Recommended Hotels

Many of the large Yugoslav-era hotels were designed for the mass market and equipped with excellent sports facilities. Despite their impersonal 1970s façades, these have been upgraded to provide such extras as wellness centres and business facilities. Small family-run hotels and tourist farms offer more personal accommodation.

The price guidelines here are for a double room with en-suite bathroom in high season (July–Aug on the coast; Dec–Jan in the ski resorts). Many hotels offer reduced rates for stays of more than three days.

€€€€€	over 180 euros
€€€€	140–180 euros
€€€	100–140 euros
€€	60–100 euros
€	below 60 euros

LJUBLJANA

Austria Trend Hotel €€€€ *Dunajska 160, tel: 01-588 25 00, www.austria-trend.at.* North of the train station, near the trade-fair complex, this hi-tech designer hotel has 214 spacious rooms and suites, each with a LCD-screen cable TV and free internet access. Other facilities include a casino and an oriental-style wellness centre.

Celica Youth Hostel € *Metelkova 8, tel: 01-230 97 00, www.souhostel.com.* Possibly the most beautifully designed youth hostel in Europe, the 20 cells of this former prison were artistically renovated to provide double rooms and dormitories. Facilities include a café, exhibition space, internet corner and a meditation room. It's so special there are guided tours daily at 2pm. Reservations essential.

City Hotel €€€ *Dalmatinova 15, tel: 01-239 00 00, www.cityhotel.si.* Near the train station, each room has satellite TV, telephone and internet access. The apartments have a separate living and sleeping area, a/c, a mini-kitchen and a working space. Facilities include a restaurant, bicycles to rent and a conference hall.

Emonec €€ *Wolfova 12, tel: 01-200 15 20, www.hotel-emonec.com.* Lying between Kongresni trg and Prešernov trg, the 2-star Emonec is the best cheap option in the city centre. Basic but friendly. Facilities include bicycles to rent, an internet corner and a meeting room, but there is no restaurant.

Grand Hotel Union €€€€€ *Miklošičeva 1–3, tel: 01-308 12 70, www.gh-union.si.* The capital's top luxury hotel, the Union lies a few minutes' walk from the Triple Bridge. The original block is an elegant white Secessionist-style building dating from 1905. Facilities include an indoor rooftop pool, fitness centre, sauna and massage, boutique, jewellers, and hairdressers.

Mons Hotel €€€€€ *Pot za Brdom 4, tel: 01-470 27 00, www.hotel.mons.si.* Located near the ring road, this ultra-modern hotel has double-height glass windows and glass-sided corridors with woodland views. Air conditioning starts automatically when you close a window, and each room has a commissioned piece of art. There are two restaurants, a cocktail bar and four conference rooms, and free bus transfers to the city centre.

Pri Mraku €€€ *Rimska 4, tel: 01-421 96 00, www.daj-dam.si.* Located in a side street near the Križanke Summer Theatre, this 3-star hotel has 30 rooms, each with en-suite bathroom, cable TV, telephone, internet access, hairdryer and safe. Some but not all rooms have air conditioning. Facilities include a restaurant with a garden open for outdoor dining throughout summer, plus an internet corner.

NORTHWEST

BLED

Bledec Youth Hostel € *Grajska 17, tel: 04-574 52 50, www.youth-hostel-bledec.si.* This upmarket youth hostel is on the hill above the lake, on the way to the castle. All rooms have wooden floors and dark wood furniture. Facilities include a restaurant with an open-air terrace, and a common room with internet.

Garni Pension Berc €€ *Želeška cesta 15, tel: 04-574 18 38, www.berc-sp.si.* Set in a lovely garden just a few minutes' walk from the lake, this former farmhouse, dating back to 1848, offers a warm, homely atmosphere. Each of the 11 rooms has a pine ceiling, a balcony, en-suite bathroom, cable TV and telephone.

Grand Hotel Toplice €€€€€ *Cesta svobode 20, tel: 04-579 10 00, www.hotel-toplice.com.* Dating back to 1875, the rooms in this luxury hotel are furnished with antiques, all have balconies and most command views of the lake. The impressive wellness centre includes an indoor pool filled with thermal water, a sauna, and beauty salon.

Vila Bled €€€€€ *Cesta svobode 26, tel: 04-579 15 00, www.vilabled.com.* This elegant retreat, once Tito's summer villa, is set in peaceful parkland giving onto the lake, a 20-minute walk from the centre. All rooms and suites retain their period 1950s furnishing. Wellness centre, tennis court and a private lido with rowing boats.

BOHINJ

Hotel Jezero €€ *Ribčev Laz 51, 04-572 91 00, www.bohinj.si/alpinum/jezero/.* This modern, alpine-style hotel commands a prime site at the east end of Lake Bohinj, Most of the rooms have balconies. Indoor pool, sauna, gymnasium and an internet corner.

Vila Park €€€ *Ukanc 129, tel: 04-572 33 00, www.vila-park.com.* At the west end of Lake Bohinj, this small hotel is in a beautiful garden with a stream and views of the mountains where guests can dine in summer. Each of the seven chic double rooms has internet access, TV and safe. Facilities include a sauna, bar and restaurant.

BOVEC

Hotel Mangart €€€ *Mala vas 107, tel: 05-388 42 50, www.hotel-mangart.com.* A recently built hotel with a beautiful mountain backdrop, Hotel Mangart has 34 standard and 2 deluxe rooms, all with satellite TV, phone and internet access, and most with a balcony. Wellness facilities include whirlpool, sauna and massages.

KRANJSKA GORA

Hotel Kotnik €€ *Borovška 75, tel: 04-588 15 64, www.hotel-kotnik.si.* Close to the main square, this two-storey yellow building offers 15 simple but comfortable rooms with traditional furnishing. The adjoining restaurant serves delicious pizza from a brick oven.

Kompas Hotel €€€€€ *Borovška 100, tel: 04-589 21 00, www.hit.si.* This smartly refurbished 1970s hotel lies at the foot of the ski slopes. The best rooms are the 45 superiors, each with a balcony and mountain view, plus internet access. Excellent sports facilities include a pool, gym, clay tennis courts, and mountain bikes to rent.

KOBARID

Hotel Hvala €€€ *Trg svobode 1, tel: 05-389 93 00, www.hotel-hvala.si.* One of Slovenia's most highly regarded hotels, the family-run Hvala has 28 rooms with sleek Italian furniture, plus three apartments, one for guests with mobility difficulties. Facilities include a sauna, bikes and dental care, and the outstanding Topli Val restaurant. Former guests include Michael Palin.

NOVA GORICA

Hotel Casino Perla €€€€€ *Kidričeva 7, Nova Gorica, tel: 05-331 13 41, www.thecasinoperla.com.* The vast Perla, one of the largest casinos in Europe (with 24-hour roulette, blackjack, poker and slot machines) has 225 rooms and 24 suites, plus a comprehensive wellness centre with a pool and gym.

TRENTA VALLEY

Pristava Lepena €€€ *Lepena 2, Soča, tel: 05-388 99 00, www.pristava-lepena.com.* On a green plateau overlooking the Soča Valley, this is a holiday village of traditional alpine cottages for a total of 50 guests. Each unit has an open fire, terrace, bathroom, phone and internet connection and TV. There is a restaurant, equestrian centre, pool, gym, sauna and a tennis court.

SOUTHWEST

IDRIJA

Kendov Dvorec €€€€€ *Spodnje Idrija, 4km (2.5 miles) from Idrija, tel: 05-372 51 00, www.kendov-dvorec.com.* One of the most exclusive hideaways in Slovenia, this restored 14th-century manor house has 11 individually designed rooms furnished with 19th-century antiques, plus a highly regarded restaurant serving local specialities. Popular honeymoon get-away. Book well in advance.

LIPICA

Hotel Klub €€€ *Lipica 5, tel: 05-739 15 80, www.lipica.org.* Set close to the peaceful green pastures of the Lipica Stud Farm, this 1980s atrium-style building has 59 rooms, each with an en-suite bathroom. Facilities include a gym, sauna, a restaurant and a bar.

PIRAN

Hotel Tartini €€€ *Tartinijev trg 15, tel: 05-671 10 00, www.hotel-tartini-piran.com.* This delightful 45-room hotel commands a prime spot beside Piran's beautiful oval-shaped piazza and harbour. The rooftop terrace has a small pool.

Val Hostel € *Gregorčičeva 38a, Piran, tel: 05-673 25 55, www.hostel-val.com.* Perfectly located in the heart of the old town, this highly regarded hostel has 22 rooms totalling 56 beds, with shared bathrooms on each floor. Facilities include a kitchen, laundry, restaurant, TV and internet corner.

PORTOROŽ

Grand Hotel Portorož €€€€€ *Obala 43, Portorož, tel: 05-696 90 01, www.lifeclass.net.* This modern 5-star hotel overlooks the seafront promenade. A vast spa offers treatments using brine, mud and algae from the local saltpans, thermal water pools, sauna, Thai massage and a fitness centre. Hotel guests have reduced rates in the spa.

NORTHEAST

LOGAR VALLEY

Hotel Plesnik €€€€ *Logarska dolina 10, Solčava, tel: 03-839 23 00, www.plesnik.si.* This up-market, 4-star hotel makes a romantic escape for exploring the green meadows of Logar Valley. Housed in an Alpine-style building, it has 30 double rooms, most with a balcony and spectacular mountain views, plus a bar, restaurant, swimming pool, sauna, whirlpool, solarium and massage.

MARIBOR

Hotel Orel €€€ *Volkmerjev prehod 7, tel: 02-250 67 00, www.termemb.si.* Ideally located in the old town, the 3-star Orel has 80 guest rooms with smart en-suite bathrooms, and there's a fine ground-floor restaurant.

Hotel Piramida €€€€ *Ulica Heroja Šlandra 10, tel: 02-234 44 00, www.termemb.si.* Located between the old town and the train and bus stations, this smart, functional six-storey hotel has 70 well-equipped guest rooms, bar, restaurant, and a business centre.

MORAVSKE TOPLICE

Hotel Livada Prestige €€€€ *Kranjčeva 12, Moravske Toplice, tel: 02-512 50 55, www.terme3000.si.* This ultra-modern 5-star hotel has 119 rooms and suites, each with a spring of genuine 'black' thermomineral water. Facilities include indoor and outdoor pools, a restaurant, bar and conference facilities. Guests can use the Livada Golf Course in the complex.

PTUJ

Hotel Mitra €€€ *Prešernova ulica 6, tel: 02-787 74 55, www.hotel-mitra.si.* In the heart of the old town this romantic, old-fashioned hotel dates from 1870. It has 21 comfortable rooms and two suites, furnished with reproduction antiques, plus restaurant.

ROGAŠKA SLATINA

Grand Hotel Sava €€€€ *Zdravliški trg 6, tel: 03-811 40 00, www.rogaska.si.* Amid manicured gardens and connected to the Drinking Hall by covered passage, this 4-star hotels' facilities include the luxurious 'Lotus Wellness Centre' and the 'Lotus Spa' (free for guests), a children's pool, plus Turkish and Finnish saunas.

Hotel Strossmayer €€€ *Zdravliški trg 14, tel: 03-811 20 00, www.terme-rogaska.si.* Dating from 1848, this grand old building retains much of its Habsburgian charm. There are 55 double rooms, 17 singles and three suites. The building is connected to the Drinking Hall by covered walkways.

SOUTHEAST

ČATEŽ

Hotel Toplice €€€€€ *Topliska 35, tel: 07-493 50 23, www.terme-catez.si.* The newest of four hotels connected to Slovenia's largest spa, Hotel Toplice combines a 1925 alpine chalet with a modern annexe. Facilities include a restaurant and bar and tennis courts.

MOKRICE

Mokrice Castle Golf Hotel €€€€€ *Rajec 4, Jesenice na Dolenjskem, tel: 07-493 50 00, www.terme-catez.si.* Lying 8km (5 miles) southeast of Čatež, this fairy-tale Renaissance castle, set in parkland houses an antique-furnished luxury hotel. There is an upmarket restaurant and an 18-hole golf course.

OTOČEC

Otočec Castle Hotel €€€€ *Grajska 2, Otočec ob Krki, tel: 07-384 89 00, www.terme-krka.si.* Lying 7km (4 miles) east of Novo mesto, the hotel is in a 13th-century Gothic-Renaissance castle, on an island on the River Krka. All rooms have period furniture. There is a golf course and an equestrian centre nearby.

INDEX

Berlitz pocket guide

Slovenia

Third Edition 2012
Reprinted 2013

Written by Jane Foster
Updated by Bill Hemsley
Edited by Paula Soper
Commissioned by Pamela Afram
Series Editor: Tom Stainer

Printed by CTPS-China

Berlitz Trademark Reg. U.S. Patent Office and other countries. Marca Registrada. Used under licence from the Berlitz Investment Corporation

Photography credits
Neil Buchan-Grant/APA 3CR, 5BR, 11, 12, 14, 15, 19, 21, 26, 30, 32, 33, 34, 35, 36, 37, 64, 66, 75, 77, 79, 81, 83, 92, 93, 94, 96, 106; iStockphoto 23, 41, 102, 103; PjrFoto.com/Phil Robinson/ Alamy 16; Slovenia.info 2T, 3TR, 4–5, 4B, 4TR, 5B, 5TR, 8, 24, 28, 39, 42, 45, 47, 48, 53, 54, 57, 61, 63, 69, 70, 71, 84, 87, 89, 99; Slovenian Government Public Relations and Media Office 52; Gregory Wrona 9, 17, 20, 31, 51, 55, 58, 59, 68, 73, 76, 80, 100, 104, 105

Cover picture: 4Corners Images

Every effort has been made to provide accurate information in this publication, but changes are inevitable. The publisher cannot be responsible for any resulting loss, inconvenience or injury.

Contact us

At Berlitz we strive to keep our guides as accurate and up to date as possible, but if you find anything that has changed, or if you have any suggestions on ways to improve this guide, then we would be delighted to hear from you.

Berlitz Publishing, PO Box 7910, London SE1 1WE, England.
email: berlitz@apaguide.co.uk
www.insightguides.com/berlitz